The Illustrated Encyclopedia of Carpentry & Woodworking Tools, Terms & Materials

by Stanley Schuler

PEQUOT PRESS / RANDOM HOUSE

Chester, Conn.   New York

Other books by Stanley Schuler

How to Fix Almost Everything

All Your Home Building and Remodeling Questions
Answered

The Home Owner's Minimum Maintenance Manual

Complete Book of Closets and Storage

ISBN: 0-394-70661-7
Library of Congress Catalog Number: 72-12225

Manufactured in the United States of America

First Edition

HOW TO USE THIS BOOK

Like all encyclopedias, this book lists items in alphabetical order. When several fall under a single generic name, they are so listed: all saws at SAW, HAND; all joints at JOINT. Cross references are included under the specific name:

> RIP SAW. See *saw.*
> CHAIR RAIL. See *molding.*
> BUTT JOINT. See *joint.*

Illustrations are placed immediately after, or within, the pertinent entry.

A

ABRASIVE. An abrasive is a material used for smoothing wood or taking it down a fraction of an inch. The most common abrasives (discussed under separate entries) are *sandpaper* and *steel wool*. Others are *Carborundum, emery cloth, Stanbrite, bronze wool, pumice* and *rottenstone*.

Whatever the abrasive you are using, you should always work with the grain to prevent scratching of the surface.

ACROSS THE GRAIN. Term used when working lumber at an angle more or less perpendicular to the direction of the grain. See *with the grain*.

ADJUSTABLE SPRING CATCH. See *catch*.

ADZ. An axe-like tool used to rough-dress large timbers. The slightly curved cutting blade is at right angles to the handle—like the blade on a mattock or the claw on a hammer. When working with an adz, you stand straddling the timber and swing the tool down toward you on to the top surface of the wood.

AFRICAN CHERRY. See *makori*.

AFRICAN MAHOGANY. Not a true mahogany but a beautiful pink to reddish-brown hardwood, usually with pronounced figuring and high luster. It is fairly hard but easy to work. It goes into fine furniture and decorative plywood.

AFRICAN TEAK. See *iroko*.

AFRICAN WALNUT. See *tigerwood*.

AFRORMOSIA. A hard, heavy, strong African hardwood used in furniture, wall paneling and ship decks. Resembling teak, it has a straight grain with some mottle. The color is a warm brown with yellow-brown bands.

AGAINST THE GRAIN. See *with the grain*.

AGBA. A West African furniture wood suggestive of African mahogany. It is a pale reddish-brown, straight-grained, light, soft and easily worked.

AIR-DRIED LUMBER. Lumber which is seasoned simply by allowing air to circulate around it. The resulting lumber is every bit as good as kiln-dried lumber if the seasoning is done properly and is not hurried.

Whichever seasoning process is used, the moisture content of rough boards and timbers less than 8 in. wide used in construction should not exceed 19 percent; that of wider lumber should not exceed 15 per cent. Finish lumber should have an even lower moisture content.

ALDER. Of the various species of alder, only the red alder of the Pacific Northwest is used for lumber, and that to only a limited extent in plywood and structural parts of furniture. It is white to pinkish-brown in color, of medium weight, and with mediocre characteristics.

ALL-N-ONE MEASURING TOOL. See *square*.

AMARANTH. A strong, tough, heavy Central American hardwood used in furniture veneers and art objects. An alternate name is purpleheart. It is brown when cut but almost immediately turns rich purple.

AMBOYNA. A rose-red wood with little bird's-eye knots, growing in the East Indies, is used in inlays and small objects. It is very hard and dense.

ANGLE DIVIDER. See *divider*.

ANGLE IRON. Also called angle brace, a sturdy steel or brass strip bent at a right angle. It is used to reinforce corners formed by two pieces of wood butted together, as at the corners of picture frames or window screens. One type of angle iron, called a flat corner brace, is screwed flat to the wood. Another type, called a corner brace, is set inside the corner between the pieces of wood.

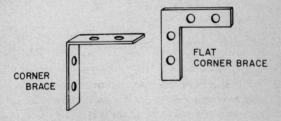

CORNER BRACE

FLAT CORNER BRACE

ANIMAL GLUE. See *glue*.

ANNULAR RING. The annual growth ring of a tree. See *growth ring*.

APPLE. A hard, close-grained, light-colored wood looking so much like birch that experts have trouble distinguishing between them. It is used for turning and carving.

APPLIED ORNAMENT. A decorative detail that is made separately and then applied to a piece of furniture, cabinet or house.

APRON. A horizontal board set on edge under the front edge of a flat surface. The piece of trim nailed to the wall underneath a windowsill is called an apron. Similarly, the boards below the outside edges of many table tops are aprons.

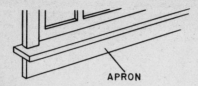

APRON

ARBOR. The shaft to which a rotating tool, such as a circular saw blade, is attached.

ARRIS. The sharp edge, ridge or hip formed when two pieces of wood meet at an outside corner.

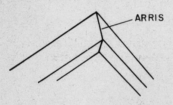

ARRIS

ASH. Several species of ash are used in making furniture and handles. The wood is very hard, tough and heavy. It is light grayish-brown with white sapwood and a pronounced figure.

ASPEN. See *poplar*.

ASTRAGAL. A decorative molding used to cover joints in paneled walls and ceilings, and between double doors.

AUGER. A T-shaped tool for drilling large holes. The steel bit is driven into wood by slowly turning the handle at the top in windlass fashion.

AUGER BIT. See *bit*.

AUSTRALIAN MAPLE. A very strong, lustrous wood with a pinkish-red color and pleasant aroma. It is used in fine furniture, paneling and boats. It is not a true maple.

AUTUMNWOOD. More commonly called summerwood, it is the woody growth made by trees during the summer. See *summerwood*.

AVODIRE. A choice African cabinet wood ranging from white to creamy yellow. It has a satiny luster and mottled figure.

AWL. A small, sharp-pointed instrument like an icepick. It is used for making screwholes when you don't want to bother with a drill. You also use it to draw lines on a piece of wood where pencil lines might be erased.

AXE. Although axes are essential tools, they are not widely used by carpenters or woodworkers. You might, however, use a broadaxe for hewing timbers for a log cabin or other rustic structure. The broadaxe has a very wide blade for dressing the sides of timbers.

Conventional (single-edge) axes have smaller heads and are used for felling trees and splitting logs. The smallest size has a 1-1/2 lb. head and a short handle, and is wielded with one hand. Carpenters sometimes use it instead of a hatchet to rough-dress or point lumber. The largest single-edge axe has a 5-lb. head and a long handle for two-handed use. Double-edge axes also have long handles. They are used almost exclusively by lumbermen.

B

BACK-FLAP HINGE. See *hinge*.

BACKSAW. See *saw, hand*.

BALUSTER. One of the small uprights in a stair railing or balustrade.

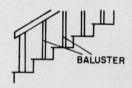

BAND CLAMP. See *clamp*.

BANDING. A narrow border around a table top, drawer front, etc. It may be an inlay, a small molding, or almost anything.

BANDSAW. See *saw, shop*.

BANISTER. Incorrect name for a baluster. Banister is the name sometimes applied to the entire railing on a stairway. It also applies to the splats forming the back of a banister-back chair.

BAR CLAMP. See *clamp*.

BARK POCKET. A piece of bark enclosed in the wood.

BARREL BOLT. See *bolt*.

BASEBOARD. A flat piece of trim nailed to an interior wall just above the floor line. An ornamental base-cap molding is usually nailed to the wall above the baseboard, and the joint at the floor line is covered with a quarter-round molding called the base shoe. In some cases, however, the baseboard and base-cap molding are one piece of wood.

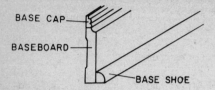

BASE-CAP MOLDING. See *molding*.

BASSWOOD. Called a hardwood, but actually quite soft and light in weight. The wood is creamy-white, has very little grain and is one of the easiest woods to work. It is used primarily for furniture parts. The tree known to gardeners as the linden is a basswood.

BASTARD-SAWED. Hardwood lumber that has a mixed grain. See *grain*.

BATTEN. Normally a narrow strip of wood used to cover the joint between two vertical boards. See *board and batten*. A cleat nailed across one or more boards to prevent warping is also called a batten.

BATTER. The backward slope sometimes given to a wall, either on purpose or by accident. It corresponds to the pitch of a roof.

BEAD. A small, convex molding that usually has some simple, repeated ornamentation. It can be referred to as beading. A bead is also a continuous, smooth convex strip plowed into a board, such as a ceiling board, for ornamentation.

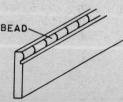

BEAM. A large timber installed horizontally and used to support a load, such as the floor of a house. Beams are at least 5 in. thick. Their width is at least 2 in. more than their thickness.

BEARER STRIP. The wood strip on which the front of a drawer rests when closed.

BEARING PARTITION. A wall that carries some of the weight of the joists above it. All exterior walls are bearing partitions though they are not known as such. As a rule, only a few of the interior walls are bearing partitions.

BEDPLATE. A horizontal timber or metal slab placed under a structural support to spread the load. For example, posts under girders are commonly supported by bedplates.

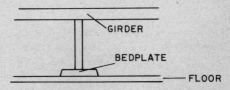

BEECH. A very hard, very tough, heavy, close-grained wood that bends well and easily. Its color ranges from white to pale brown. It is used in furniture and flooring; and, because it has very little taste or odor, it is often used in woodenware.

BENCH HOOK. A board with a wood cleat nailed across one end. It is sometimes used instead of a vise to hold small pieces of wood stationary while being sawed. With the bench hook placed cleat-side up, one hand holds the

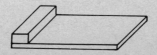

workpiece against the cleat while the other hand uses the saw.

A bench hook is also used cleat-side down with the cleat hooked over the edge of the workbench. This provides a slightly raised platform to support pieces being cut with a back saw.

BENCH RULE. See *rule*.

BENCH SAW. See *saw, shop*.

BENCH STOP. A steel or wooden device with a spring on one side. It is set into holes in top of a workbench and used to brace boards as you plane them.

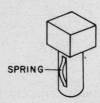

SPRING →

BENCH VISE. See *vise*.

BENGE. A brown-striped hardwood with strong figure used in plywood paneling. It comes from Africa.

BENIN. A furniture and paneling wood. It is sometimes called tigerwood because in its best form it has a yellow background with black ribbon stripes of varying widths.

BENTWOOD. Wood which has been steamed until soft and then bent into special shapes. The word is applied particularly to a type of furniture usually made of beech, but other articles such as hockey sticks are also bentwood.

BEVEL. A tool for checking and marking angles. It consists of a flat steel blade that slides and pivots in a handle with a locking screw. Blades range from 6 to 12 in. long.

The angle of the bevel is set either with a protractor

or by fitting the bevel to a piece of wood or a wooden part that has already been beveled.

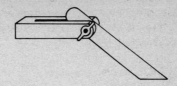

BEVEL. To cut the edge of a board or timber at an angle. Also a board edge trimmed to any angle. Compare *chamfer*.

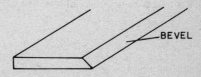

BEVEL SIDING. A wedge-shaped board, thicker along one edge than the other. When applied horizontally to an exterior wall, the thicker edge is at the bottom and overlaps the thinner top edge of the board below. Clapboards and shingles are familiar forms of bevel siding.

BIRCH. The wood of both the yellow birch and the sweet, or black, birch. They are used in cabinets, furniture, paneling and millwork. The two woods are similar: hard, heavy, tough, and with a close grain. The heartwood is reddish-brown; the sapwood, white. The birch lumber sold as "select" is more uniform in color than that labeled "unselect", but there is no difference otherwise.

BIRD CAGE. The cage-like blocks that permit a tilt-top table to tilt and rotate.

BIRD'S-EYE MAPLE. See *maple*.

BIRD'S MOUTH. A triangular cut made near the lower end of a rafter to fit over the rafter plate.

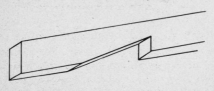

BIT. Rotating cutting tool used in bit braces, hand drills or drill presses for boring holes.

Auger bits are the type most often used in bit braces (and large-size bits of this type are sometimes used in electric drills). The square tang at the top of the bit is held in the jaws of the brace. The small screw point at the bottom is the feed screw that pulls the bit into the wood. Actual cutting is done by the vertical cutters, called spurs, on either side of the feed screw, and by horizontal cutters, called cutting edges.

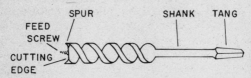

The auger bits most often used are from 7 to 10 in. long, but you can get 5-in. bits for making dowel holes and 18- to 24-in. bits for heavy construction.

Auger bits are sized by sixteenths of an inch and range from 1/4- to 2-in. diameter. The bit size is stamped on the shank. A 7 stands for 7/16-in. diameter; 12 for 12/16-in., or 3/4-in., diameter; 20 for 20/16-in., or 1-1/4-in., diameter.

The thread size of the feed screw also varies between bits. The so-called single thread is designed for rough carpentry work; the double thread, for fine work.

Expansive bits are used in bit braces to cut holes from 7/8- to 3-in. diameter. They have a square shank at the top; a feed screw at the bottom. A single adjustable cutter extending to one side of the feed screw removes wood in sizable chips.

Twist drills or drill bits, are the mainstays of anyone using an electric drill or drill press. They are short and V-nosed, and have a round shank that is locked into the chuck by hand or, in better drills, with a chuck key. Bits are available for boring holes of from 1/16- to 1/2-in. diameter. An electrician's bit similar to a twist drill is available in 3/4-in. diameter.

Twist drills are normally the same diameter from end to end; but large drills designed for use in 1/4-in. chucks are reduced to 1/4-in. diameter at the shank end.

To save money, most craftsmen buy twist drills that will drill wood as well as metal. These are made of heat-treated high-speed steel. But drills of carbon-steel are available for use on wood only.

Power-bore bits and *flat power bits* are designed for drilling holes of from 3/8 to 1-1/2 in. diameter. Both fit 1/4-in. drills. The former has a flat, horizontal cutting head with a sharp point and is the more suitable for careful precision work. The latter has a flat, spade-like, vertical cutting head with a sharp point. It is better for rough work because it tends to splinter wood if not properly used.

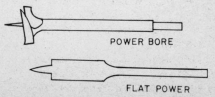

POWER BORE

FLAT POWER

Lock-set bits resemble power-bore bits but are available in sizes up to 2-1/8 in. They have a hexagonal shank and can be used in either electric drills or bit braces.

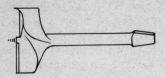

Foerstner bits resemble a power-bore bit without a feed screw. They are used in bit braces and electric drills when you want to drill a hole almost through wood without breaking it on the back side. They are also used when an auger bit might splinter wood. Sizes range from 1/4-in. to 2-in. diameter.

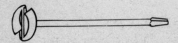

Self-feed bits drill holes from 1-3/4- to 2-9/16 in. diameter. They have flat cutting heads with ripsaw-like teeth.

BIT BRACE. A hand tool for boring holes—usually rather large holes. At the bottom end is a chuck to hold auger bits or expansive bits; at the top is a mushroom-shaped handle to push against when drilling; in between is a U-shaped sweep handle that is turned with the free hand.

The standard bit brace drives the bit into the wood when you turn to the right, and withdraws it when you turn to the left. A ratchet brace is used when a tight spot prevents turning the sweep handle a full revolution. With this type of brace, a cam above the chuck is used to control boring and withdrawal. If the cam is turned to the right, the bit cuts into the wood when you turn the handle to the right; remains stationary when you swing back to the left; then bites into the wood again when you turn to the right. After a hole is bored to the proper depth, you turn the cam to the left and withdraw the bit by turning the handle again and again to the left.

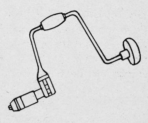

An unusual type of bit brace called a *corner brace* is used to bore holes in corners against walls, floors and beams. In this, the chuck is set at an angle to the sweep.

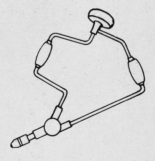

BIT EXTENSION. Rod-like device designed to let you drill holes in cramped spaces or to unusual depths. One style is used in a bit brace; the other in a 1/4-in. electric drill.

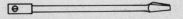

BIT GAUGE. See *gauge*.

BLACKBEAN. A coarse-grained Australian wood resembling chestnut. It ranges from dark to light brown and is shaded with still lighter brown. It looks oily. The principal use is as a veneer for furniture and interior paneling.

BLACK WALNUT. See *walnut*.

BLEEDING. Wood is said to bleed when the resin or soluble salts in it stain paint on the surface. Knots in resinous wood such as pine are particularly prone to bleed. In fact, it is wise always to assume that they will, and coat them with a knot-sealer before applying the final finish. However, cedar and redwood contain salts which also bleed, causing splotchy stains, if moisture gets into them.

BLEMISH. An imperfection which detracts from the appearance of wood but does not affect it otherwise. By contrast, a defect is an imperfection that impairs the utility of wood.

BLOCK. A small piece of wood used as a brace. For instance, a rectangular block is sometimes set into the corner of a box to strengthen it. A triangular block is glued under a stair tread to hold it to the riser. A notched triangular block is sometimes screwed under table tops and chair seats to keep the legs from wobbling.

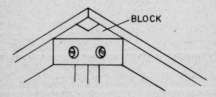

BLOCK

BLOCK FLOORING. See *flooring*.

BLOCK PLANE. See *plane*.

BLUE STAIN. A bluish or grayish stain caused by fungi in unseasoned lumber. It has no effect on the strength or durability of the lumber, but mars its appearance.

BOARD. A piece of lumber which has a nominal thickness of 1 in. and a nominal width of 2 in. or more.

BOARD AND BATTEN. A type of exterior siding made of wide, vertical boards with narrow battens covering the joints to keep out water. In batten and board siding, the battens are placed behind the boards. Boats are also constructed in the latter way. This is called batten seam construction.

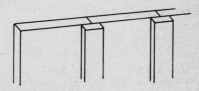

BOARD FOOT. The standard unit of measure for most lumber. A board foot is 1 in. thick, 12 in. wide and 1 ft. long. To find the number of board feet in a piece of lumber, multiply the nominal thickness in inches by the nominal width in inches by the length in feet and divide by 12. For example, to find the board feet in a piece 1 in. by 8 in. by 12 ft.—

$$\frac{1 \times 8 \times 12}{12} = 8 \text{ board feet}$$

To find the board feet in a piece 2 in. by 6 in. by 16 ft.—

$$\frac{2 \times 6 \times 16}{12} = 16 \text{ board feet}$$

BOARD MEASURE. The system for measuring lumber by board feet.

BOLT. Nuts and bolts are used to fasten wood to wood, and wood to other materials, when you want a secure union that can be broken only with a wrench.

When using any type of bolt, it is necessary first to drill a hole the size of the shank. Flat washers may be inserted under the head of the bolt and/or the nut to keep them from being drawn into the wood. When such a washer is used under the nut, it is advisable to insert between them a lock washer to prevent loosening of the nut. See *washer*.

Stove bolts are small bolts threaded from end to end and with screwdriver slots cut in the round or flat heads. They are made in diameters of 1/8 to 1/2 in. and in lengths from 3/8 to 6 in.

Carriage bolts have smooth, round heads with square collars underneath to keep the bolts from turning in wood or metal. Between the collars and the threads are smooth shanks. The bolts are made in 3/16- to 3/4-in. diameters and in lengths from 3/4 to 20 in.

Machine bolts have square or hexagonal heads which are turned with a wrench and smooth shanks above the threads. Diameters range from 3/16 to 1-1/4 in.; lengths, from 3/4 to 39 in.

BOLT, LOCKING. Simple device for locking doors, windows and cabinets.

Barrel bolt is surface-mounted and has a sliding bolt which slips into a barrel-like loop screwed to the door casing.

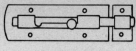

BARREL BOLT

Cremorne bolt, a related device used on French doors to secure them simultaneously at top and bottom, is closed and opened by a central knob actuating long rods on either side.

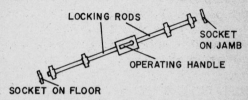

Foot bolt another related device, is used to lock doors at the bottom. You close it by stepping on the top of the bolt. To open it, you step on a trigger on the side of the bolt housing. This releases the bolt, which is then retracted by a wire spring.

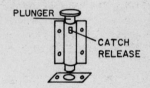

Mortise bolt is contained in a sleeve which is mortised into the edge of a door or window. It slips into a strikeplate in the jamb when actuated by a knob on the door or window surface.

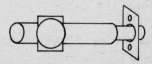

BOSS. A small ornament such as a rosette or keystone which is applied to a surface.

BOX NAIL. See *nail*.

BOXWOOD. A dense, close-grained, very hard, extremely heavy wood. Ranging from almost white to deep yellow, it is used for small turnings and carvings.

BRACE. A piece of wood or metal used to strengthen a member or part of a structure, furniture piece, etc. For example, when two pieces of wood come together in a corner, an easy way to strengthen the corner is to nail a third piece of wood diagonally across it. This is the brace.

A table giving the lengths of braces for various situations is included on the back of the tongue of a framing square.

For the tool used to bore holes, see *bit brace*.

BRACKET. A device projecting from a vertical surface which is used to support a weight, such as a shelf, cornice, handrail or ladder which is not in use. An angle iron is a familiar type of bracket.

BRAD. Small, thin finishing nail used for many purposes in carpentry and cabinetwork. Ranging from 1/2 to 1-1/2 in. long, brads are graded by their length, not by the penny system used for larger nails.

BRAD AND NAIL DRIVER. A tool for driving brads and finishing nails which are too small to hold or are in an awkward position. You insert a brad into the hollow steel tip of the tool, then pump the screwdriver-like wood handle at the back up and down.

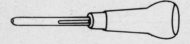

BREAST DRILL. See *drill*.

BRIDGING. The braces installed between joists to stiffen them, hold them in alignment and distribute floor loads. Normally bridging is made of two boards 3- or 4-in. wide nailed between adjacent joists to form an X. This is called cross-bridging to differentiate it from solid-bridging, made with short lengths of joist lumber.

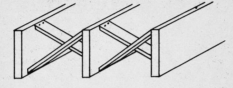

BRONZE WOOL. An abrasive material similar to steel wool but made of bronze. It should be used instead of steel wool when you are finishing boats and other articles that will be in contact with water, because particles that become embedded in the wood will not rust and cause stains.

BUBINGA. A heavy, hard West African furniture or paneling wood with a pale violet background and evenly spaced purple lines. It is usually highly figured.

BUNGALOW SIDING. Another name for Colonial siding.

BURL. An abnormal, more or less dome-shaped growth on a tree trunk that can be cut into thin slices to make an unusual, often very beautiful veneer.

Conventional lumber cut from a trunk which contains a burl often shows a distortion of grain. Such a blemish is also known as a burl.

BURNISHER. An awl-like tool with a very tough steel blade for turning the edges on scraper blades.

BUTT. To place or fasten one thing against another. For example, at the corner of a building, one sill timber is butted against the other at right angles.

Carpenters also refer to butt hinges simply as butts.

BUTT CHISEL. See *chisel, wood*.

BUTTERNUT. Butternut is an American walnut much like black walnut but with lighter-colored wood. It is sometimes called white walnut. The wood is fairly soft and light, with a fine grain. It is used in furniture and cabinet work.

BUTT GAUGE. See *gauge*.

BUTT HINGE. See *hinge*.

BUTT JOINT. See *joint*.

BUTT MARKER. A cutting tool which is held against the edge of a door or a jamb and struck with a mallet to cut the edges of a butt-hinge mortise.

CUTTING
EDGES

C

CABINET CHISEL. See *chisel, wood*.

CABINET SCRAPER. See *scraper*.

CABIN HOOK. A type of hook and eye used on cabinets. The hook is pinned in place so that it moves up and down at all times parallel to the door to which it is attached.

CALIPERS. An instrument for measuring inside and outside dimensions of round, oval, irregular, etc. objects which are difficult to measure with a rule.

Calipers used for making outside measurements are shaped like a compass but have bowed legs with the points turned in toward each other. For making inside measurements, calipers have straight legs with the points turned out away from each other. In both cases, you need a rule to measure the distance between the points.

INSIDE   OUTSIDE

A caliper rule is used for both outside and inside measurements and indicates on a 32nds of an inch scale what the measurements are. The calipers are too small, however, to measure all objects.

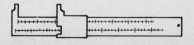

CAMBER. The slight arch given to a structure or timber to enable it to bear a load or shed water.

CANT. To set up at an angle. Also, see *flitch*.

CANTILEVER. A rigid projection from a vertical surface. A shelf bracket is a type of cantilever.

As a verb, cantilever means to build out from a vertical surface such as a wall. The word is also used as an adjective, as in cantilever shelves or cantilever balcony.

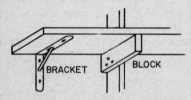

BRACKET   BLOCK

CAP. The top part of many things encountered in a structure: the cap molding at the top of a wall, the coping of a wall, the top of a column, the lintel over a window, etc.

CARBORUNDUM. A silicon-carbide abrasive commonly used in sharpening stones and grinders.

CARPENTER'S SQUARE. See *square*.

CARRIAGE. A stair stringer. See *stringer*.

CARRIAGE BOLT. See *bolt*.

CARVING. An ornament, figure, picture or decoration cut into or out of wood or other materials with knives and chisels.

CASEIN GLUE. See *glue*.

CASING. The frame nailed to the wall around a door or window. The piece across the top is called the head casing; those on either side are side casings.

CASING NAIL. See *nail*.

CASTER. A wheel to permit easy rolling of furniture and cabinets. It is installed in two ways. The stem type of caster has a round shank which is inserted in a socket set into a vertical hole drilled in the bottom of the leg. The plate type of caster has a square, flat plate which is screwed directly to the bottom of a leg.

Caster wheels for home and office duty range from 1-1/4 to 2-1/2 in. diameter, and are made of plastic, hard rubber or metal. Most are of conventional design, but a few are globular.

Much larger casters are available for shop and factory use.

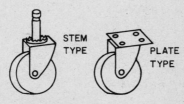

STEM TYPE

PLATE TYPE

CATCH. Device for holding cabinet and similar light-weight doors and outswinging windows closed. Catches have no locking mechanism.

Types in common use include the following:

A *friction catch* is the smallest and least obtrusive catch but also the least efficient. Used only on doors which are set into the door opening, it consists of a small button recessed in the edge of the door, and a saucer-like strikeplate fastened to the jamb.

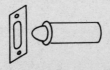

A *magnetic catch* has a magnet mounted on the jamb and a metal plate on the door.

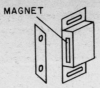

MAGNET

An *adjustable spring catch* is a device for windows and large doors. The spring section is mounted on the jamb and has an outswinging arm that engages a hook on the door.

A *double-roller spring catch* has two rollers mounted in the cabinet with a prong mounted on the door. The rollers grip the prong in pincer-fashion. In another version of this catch, two crimped pieces of spring steel take the place of the rollers.

A *single-roller spring catch* has a roller mounted on the door that engages a strikeplate on the jamb. A spring button catch is similar: as the button on the door slides up over the tent-shaped or L-shaped strikeplate, it is depressed; then pushes outward to catch on the inner strikeplate surface.

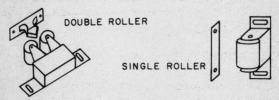

DOUBLE ROLLER

SINGLE ROLLER

A *touch catch* is essentially similar to a double-roller spring catch but releases automatically when you push the closed door.

CAULKING. A flexible material used to make joints watertight. Old types of caulking were oil-base compounds which dried out and disintegrated rather rapidly. Much improved modern types are made with latex, acrylics, rubber or silicone.

CAUL. A device used to press veneer on to a backing.

C CLAMP. See *clamp*.

CEDAR. Trees of several different genera are called cedars. All are needled evergreens having soft wood that is more or less white under the bark and red to brown at the center. The dark heartwood has considerable resistance to decay. The wood is fine-grained, not overly strong but easily worked. It is used for a variety of purposes. The wood of the American red cedar (actually juniper) is highly aromatic and is used for making mothproof closets.

CEILING BOARD. In the lumber industry this is a specific type of board milled in a decorative pattern for application to ceilings. But any kind of board could be called a ceiling board if applied in this way.

CENTER LINE. The center of an object. On a plan or drawing it is indicated by a line of alternate dots and dashes.

CENTER-MATCHED. A term applied to boards with tongues and grooves that are centered along the edges of the boards. Most, but not all, tongue and groove boards are center-matched.

CENTER PUNCH. See *punch*.

CENTER SQUARE. A small, flat, rigid metal strip shaped at one end like a reined-in horse's head. It is used for marking right angles on lumber; making small measurements; and locating the center of a circular piece such as a table top. It can also be used as a protractor to mark off angles at any point on a piece of work. See *square*.

CHAIR RAIL. See *molding*.

CHALK LINE. A piece of thin, strong cord coated with chalk, usually blue, and used to strike (mark) a visible line on a surface. As a rule, chalk lines are used only for drawing lines longer than the longest available straight board. However, plumb lines are often chalked to make short vertical lines.

CHAMFER. To remove the sharp corner along the edge of a board or timber by planing to a 45° angle. The resulting surface is also called a chamfer. Compare *bevel*.

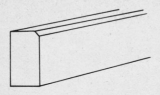

CHANNEL. A concave groove cut in wood as a decoration.

CHECK. A lengthwise crack in a piece of wood as a result of shrinkage during drying. Checks normally cross the growth rings. As they appear in logs, they are wider at the surface of the log than toward the center. Compare *heart shake*.

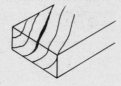

CHERRY. A hard, firm, reddish-brown hardwood widely used in cabinets, paneling and furniture because it is naturally beautiful and takes a fine polish. It has poor resistance to splitting, but in all other characteristics is rated good.

CHESTNUT. Because the American chestnut trees were wiped out many years ago by the chestnut blight, there is little chestnut lumber available today and most of that comes either from demolished buildings or dead trees. The medium-weight, grayish-brown wood has a strong figure. It is used in paneling and furniture.

CHEVRON FASTENER. A patented metal fastener for miter joints. It is a small, L-shaped strap with sharp teeth along one edge.

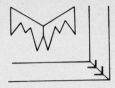

CHISEL, COLD. Heavy steel tool with integral steel handle for striking with a hammer. Designed for cutting materials much tougher than wood, it is used primarily by metalworkers and masons. Carpenters need a cold chisel only to cut heads off immovable nails, screws and bolts.

CHISEL, WOOD. Stiff, wood- or plastic-handled tool with straight, flat cutting edge used for removing chips or strips of wood. Chisels are worked with and across the grain. Depending on the density of the wood and the cut being made, they are operated either entirely by hand pressure or by striking the end of the handle with a mallet or soft-faced hammer.

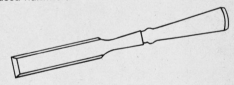

Standard wood chisels have flat blades with parallel sides. Blade widths range from 1/8 to 1-1/2 in. The overall length, including the handle, ranges from 7-3/4 to 10 in. Cabinet, or pocket, chisels are similarly designed but have slightly shorter blades to permit more accurate work. Butt chisels have still shorter blades and are used for making hinge and similar mortises. The widest butt chisel blade measures 2 in. A slick is a huge chisel with 3-in. blade used mainly in boat building for rough shaping wood.

Woodcarver's chisels range from 1/32 to 1 in. wide. From 3/4 in. up, they have tapered sides and are known as fishtail chisels. Smaller chisels have parallel sides and are called straight chisels. There are also bent chisels which are shaped at the end something like a cupped hand so that the worker can more easily get into deep and awkward areas.

Woodcarver's chisels are also given numbers which relate not to the width but the way they cut. No. 2 chisels, like all carpenter's chisels, have single-bevel cutting edges. No. 1 chisels, on the other hand, are sharpened on both sides.

CHORD. Any one of the principal timbers in a truss. Sometimes, however, the word is applied only to the long horizontal member of a truss (the joist).

CIRCLE CUTTER. A tool used in a drill press, electric drill or bit brace to cut out large circles from various materials. The cutting is done with a chisel-like, vertical bit held in an arm with a set screw. The bit can be adjusted to cut circles of different sizes.

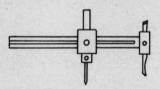

CIRCULAR PLANE. See *plane*.

CIRCULAR SAW. See *saw, portable power*.

CLAMP. Clamps are essential tools in a great many gluing operations and are also used to hold materials while you work on them.

C clamps, or carriage-maker's clamps, are rather small, C-shaped devices with an adjustable bolt through one end. Because the jaws are small, pressure is concentrated and there is danger that the wood being clamped will be dented. In using these clamps, it is therefore customary to insert pieces of wood between the jaws and the work to spread the pressure and prevent denting.

Spring clamps are like a pair of pliers with a spring that holds the jaws closed. Like C clamps, they are used for small jobs, but exert less pressure.

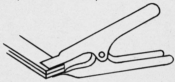

Hand screws, or screw clamps, are designed for larger jobs. They consist of two thick, parallel pieces of hardwood joined by long, parallel bolts which are screwed in opposite directions. Because the bolts are adjusted separately, the clamps are suited to work with either parallel or non-parallel surfaces.

A *bar clamp*, also called a cabinet clamp, can be used on work up to 6 ft. long. It is a long steel bar with a fixed jaw at one end and an adjustable jaw with a bolt at the other end. The latter is held in place by notches in the bar. A small version of this clamp is only 1 ft. long.

A *band clamp* is a steel strap with horns that are pulled together with a hand screw. The clamp is used on round and oval work.

A *web clamp* is a 12-ft. tape of nylon webbing with a steel fastener that is tightened with a screwdriver or wrench. It is used on round and irregular work.

A *corner clamp* is a flat triangular device used to clamp corners of furniture frames, picture frames and the like. The frame is set into the clamp, and a diagonal bolt then pushes it against the corner. In a variation of this device, pressure is exerted by two bolts, which tighten against the outside corners of the frame.

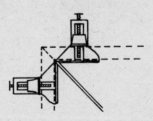

CLAPBOARD. A bevel siding 1/2 in. thick at the thickest edge and only 4 to 6 in. wide. It is applied horizontally to exterior walls.

CLAW HAMMER. See *hammer*.

CLEAT. A piece of lumber nailed to a vertical surface to support a shelf or something similar, or to serve as a base for coat hooks. A cleat is also a piece of wood attached to the back of one or more pieces of lumber to tie them together in a plane or to prevent warping.

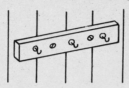

CLINCH. To bend down the point of a nail protruding from a piece of wood in order to keep it from pulling out.

COCK BEADING. A small, rounded molding used as decorative trim on furniture and cabinets.

COCOBOLO. A hard, heavy, oily Central American wood which is very difficult to glue; it is therefore used mainly for turnings and small objects. It is a mixture of red, orange and black.

COLLAR. A molding or integral raised band encircling a furniture leg, baluster, etc.

COLLAR BEAM. A horizontal, 2-in. thick timber used to tie together and stiffen the rafters on opposite sides

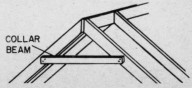

COLLAR
BEAM

of a ridge. The beam is installed several feet below the ridge and serves as a ceiling joist if the space below it is occupied.

COLONIAL SIDING. A bevel siding 3/4 in. thick at the thickest edge and from 6 to 12 in. wide. It is applied horizontally to exterior walls. Compare *clapboard*.

COMBINATION PLIERS. See *pliers*.

COMBINATION SANDER. See *sanding machine*.

COMBINATION SQUARE. See *square*.

COMMON NAIL. See *nail*.

COMMON RAFTER. See *rafter*.

COMPASS SAW. See *saw, hand*.

CONNECTOR PLATE. A small, square, flat piece of steel with several dozen short, nail-like teeth projecting from the bottom. It is used to reinforce joints in large frames, doors, etc.

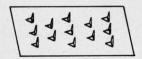

CONTACT CEMENT. See *glue*.

COPED JOINT. See *joint*.

COPING SAW. See *saw, hand*.

CORNER. A shaped brass or steel plate for protecting the corner of a chest.

CORNER BRACE. See *angle iron*. Another type of corner brace used on tables and chairs is rounded on the surface to make it more attractive. Also, see *bit brace*.

CORNER CLAMP. See *clamp*.

CORNERING TOOL. A tool for rounding off sharp edges. It is a heavy strap of steel with a slight hook incorporating a slotted cutter at each end. Each tool has two sizes of cutter.

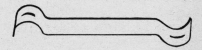

CORNICE MOLDING. See *molding*.

CORRUGATED FASTENER. Sometimes called a wiggle nail, this is a small corrugated steel strip with sharp teeth along one edge. This fastener is used to join together adjacent pieces of wood. You simply hold it upright across a joint and drive it in with a hammer until flush.

Most corrugated fasterners are straight strips roughly 1 in. long, but some are ring-shaped.

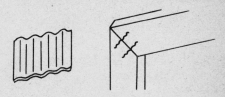

COTTONWOOD. A soft, weak hardwood used to some extent for making boxes and woodenware. It is a species of poplar.

COUNTERSINK. To sink the heads of nails, screws or bolts flush with or slightly below the surface of wood.

Nail heads are then usually covered with spackle or other filler to conceal them, prevent rusting and provide a smooth painting surface. Heads of screws and bolts may or may not be similarly covered.

Nails are countersunk with a nailset and hammer. Holes for round-head screws and bolts are made with conventional bits in a brace or electric drill. Special drill bits known as countersink bits are used for setting flat-head and oval-head screws. The oldest type of countersink bit makes a shallow, conical hole. Newer bits for use in electric drills not only make a hole for the screw head but also make a hole to the correct diameter and depth for the threads and shank. Bits for use in installing plank flooring also open a hole of proper size for the wood plug that covers the screw head.

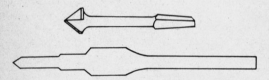

COVE MOLDING. See *molding*.

CREMORNE BOLT. See *bolt.*

CRIPPLE. A short stud or rafter.

CROSSCUT SAW. See *saw, hand*.

CROSS MEMBER. A horizontal member joining parts of a furniture piece.

CROTCH VENEER. Veneer cut from the crotch of a tree to gain a V-shaped or Y-shaped effect.

CROWN MOLDING. See *molding.*

C-SCROLL. An ornamental carving in a C shape.

CUP. A board which has curled along its length so that it is shaped like a shallow ditch is said to have a cup.

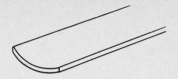

CUPBOARD CATCH. See *latch.*

CUT NAIL. See *nail.*

CYPRESS. Softwood from a deciduous southern conifer properly known as the bald cypress. The sapwood is cream colored; the heartwood, red to brown. Because of the wood's exceptional resistance to decay, it is used primarily in construction and for such things as water tanks. Wood cut from the trunk next to the buttressed roots has a crotch-like figure and is used in furniture.

D

DADO. A rectangular, across-the-grain groove into which a board is set. Setting the board is called dadoing in.

A dado is also the lower part of an interior wall which is paneled or otherwise finished in a manner different from the upper part of the wall. The two areas are commonly separated by a chair rail or other molding.

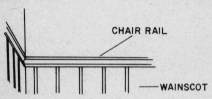

CHAIR RAIL

WAINSCOT

DADO JOINT. See *joint*.

DEAD LOAD. See *load*.

DECKING. Timbers used for roofing and flooring. They are 2 to 4 in. thick and 4 in. wide or more. Thinner boards are also used to construct decks but they are not called decking.

DEFECT. A defect in wood is an imperfection affecting the wood's utility, strength or durability. By contrast, a blemish is an imperfection that affects only the appearance of the wood.

DELAMINATE. What plywood does when the plies split apart. In modern plywood delamination is usually a problem only if an interior grade is used outdoors or is exposed to moisture.

DENTIL. One of a series of small, rectangular, tooth-like blocks in a horizontal molding. Such a molding is called a denticulated molding.

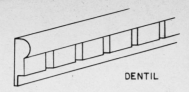

DENTIL

DEPTH GAUGE. See *gauge.*

DESIGN LOAD. See *load.*

DETAIL DRAWING. A working drawing showing precisely how specific details of a house, cabinet, furniture
piece, etc. are to be built. For example, house plans
usually include special drawings of fireplaces and stairs.
    Detail drawings are drawn to a larger scale than nor-
mal plans. In some cases, if the detail is very complicated, the drawings may be actual size.

DIMENSION LUMBER. See *lumber.*

DISK SANDER. See *sanding machine.*

DIVIDERS. Wing dividers resemble a compass with two
steel points (but in some cases, one of the points can be
replaced with a pencil). They are used for dividing, measuring, finding the center of a circle and scribing.

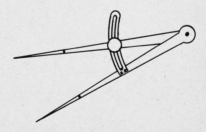

    An angle divider is a double bevel used to take off and
divide angles for mitering.

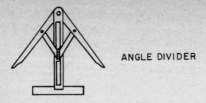

ANGLE DIVIDER

DOLLY VARDEN SIDING. A bevel siding which is rabbeted along the thick edge.

DOOR HOLDER. A plunger or arm-like device screwed to the face of a door near the bottom to hold it open.

DOOR JACK. A device made by carpenters on the job to hold doors in a true vertical position while the edges are being planed. The design varies between carpenters. A simple one consists of a horizontal timber laid on the floor with a short timber nailed perpendicular to the center and held with a brace. One end of the door rests on the horizontal timber and is clamped to the vertical timber.

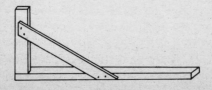

DOUBLE-ACTING HINGE. See *hinge*.

DOUBLE-HEADED NAIL. See *nail*.

DOUBLE-ROLLER SPRING CATCH. See *catch*.

DOUGLAS FIR. Douglas fir is a moderately hard soft-wood of medium weight and exceptional strength which is used almost exclusively in construction and plywood. The wood is orange-brown and variable in appearance. It is easily worked with power tools but not by hand, and must be primed carefully if it is to hold paint satisfactorily.

DOVETAIL. To fit together with an interlocking joint of this name.

DOVETAIL JOINT. See *joint*. Technically, the rectangular ends of the projections which form this type of joint are known as dovetails, while the flared sides of the projections are known as pins.

DOVETAIL SAW. See *saw, hand*.

DOWEL. A round wood or metal pin used to fasten two pieces of wood together or to strengthen a joint between two pieces. Doweling is a simple job if there is no objection to having one or both ends of the dowel showing. All you have to do is hold together the pieces to be joined, drill a hole through them, and insert a dowel of proper size. But in cases where the dowel is completely hidden, as when two boards are fastened together at the edge, it is difficult to make exactly opposite holes in a straight line without a doweling jig.

DOWELING JIG. A device to simplify the drilling of holes in two pieces of wood which are to be blind-doweled. It can be set up for dowels of several sizes, and can be used on wood up to 3 in. thick.

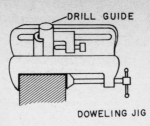

DOWELING JIG

DOWEL POINTER. A tool something like a pocket pencil sharpener with a screwdriver handle. It is used to taper the points of dowels.

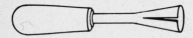

DOWEL TURNING MACHINE. A hand-operated bench tool that converts square pieces of wood into dowels. Turning a gear like that on a hand drill draws the wood through a cutter. The dowels emerge at the back end.

The machine has heads for cutting different dowel sizes.

DRAWER SLIDES. Metal tracks with rollers which are mounted on the sides or bottom of drawers to make for smoother, quieter, more reliable opening and closing. They are used mainly in kitchen cabinets.

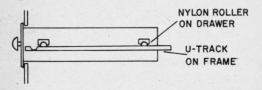

DRAWKNIFE. A tool for taking down or shaping wood longitudinally. It consists of a long, thin blade with handles at both ends and at right angles to the blade. You use the tool by pulling it toward you. It removes more

wood with each stroke than a plane but is more difficult
to control.

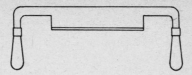

DRIFTPIN. Also called driftbolt, this is a very large steel
pin for joining timbers. Diameters measure from 1/2 to 1
in. and lengths from 18 to 26 in. Driftpins are hammered
into drilled holes of slightly smaller diameter. They
should be driven at a slight angle to the face of the wood
to impart full strength to the joint.

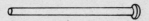

DRILL. A hand tool for drilling small holes.

Hand drills are the most common type of drill,
having a toothed gear cranked with one hand while the
other holds the tool at the proper angle and puts pres-

sure on it. The chuck holding the bit has a maximum
capacity of 1/4 or 3/8 in., depending on the model.

Breast drills have a similar drive mechanism, but
have a T-shape at the handle end to put your chest
against and exert extra pressure on the bit. One hand
turns the gear; the other grasps a handle just below the
gear on the opposite side of the central column. Breast
drills will take bits up to 1/2-in. diameter.

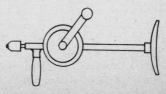

Push drills are the smallest hand drills—straight, slender devices for one-handed operation. All you do is push the handle up and down, thus rotating the bit. Drill bits up to 11/64 in. can be used.

DRILL, ELECTRIC. Ranks first in popularity among hand power tools because it performs an essential job quickly, easily, safely and at low initial cost. It can also be used for other work such as sanding, grinding, wire-brushing, buffing, countersinking and driving screws.

Most drills are pistol-shaped, with a trigger switch in the handle. A few are hammer-shaped, with the switch in the handle and a second handle on top of the motor housing.

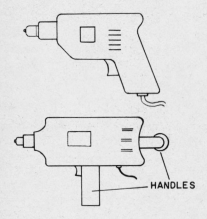

HANDLES

Drills are classified by the capacity of the chuck, the smallest being 1/4 in. Other sizes are 3/8 in., 1/2 in. and 1 in. Small sizes operate at higher speeds than large sizes and are thoroughly efficient for drilling small holes in relatively thin wood; but for drilling large holes, and for drilling in very hard or thick wood, the slower drills are preferable. Many of the drills now available operate at variable speeds.

The bits used in electric drills are described at *bit.* Other tools used include screwdriver bits, disk sanders, wire brushes, buffing wheels, grinding wheels, hole saws, Surform drums, and drill saws for cutting and shaping holes.

DRILL GUIDE. A pistol-shaped tool with a rotating dial at the front instead of a barrel. It is designed to help you make electric drill holes precisely where you want them and perpendicular to the drilled surface. It prevents the drill point from skidding from the mark.

To use the guide, you draw a cross mark where you want to make a hole. Then you rotate the dial to the correct drill size, position it over the cross mark, slip the drill through the dial hole and start drilling.

DRILL PRESS. A motor-driven shop tool which can be used not only for drilling and boring but also (if you

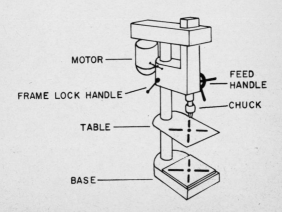

have the proper accessories) for mortising, routing, shaping, sanding, etc. The tool consists of a floor base or table with a vertical column. At the top of this is an enclosed drive mechanism and chuck. An adjustable work table is attached to the middle of the column. In operation, the entire drive mechanism, with bit inserted, is lowered on to the work on the table.

Drill presses use a wide variety of bits ranging from the smallest twist drill to the largest Foerstner bit. The drilling speed is variable.

DRILL SAW. See *saw, portable power.*

DRILL STAND. This is a heavy steel stand with a column to which a portable electric drill is clamped and used as a drill press. Like a standard drill press, the drill stand has a tilting work table. The drill rack can be raised or lowered on the column by a lever.

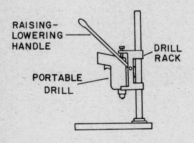

RAISING-
LOWERING
HANDLE

DRILL
RACK

PORTABLE
DRILL

DRILL STOP. See *gauge.*

DRIVE HOME. To fix a part, nail or screw in its permanent position with a hammer or screwdriver.

DROP HANDLE. A drawer pull which hangs parallel with the face of the drawer or cabinet when not in use.

DROP-LEAF HINGE. See *hinge.*

DROP-LEAF SUPPORT. A device screwed to the bottom of drop leaves on tables and folding shelves to hold them up. It is hinged in the middle and held open by a spring.

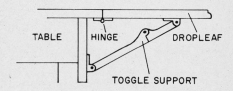

DROP SIDING. A board with a rather large concave groove along one of the front edges. When applied horizontally to an exterior wall, the groove is at the top and visually separates the board from the one above. In actuality, however, the edges of the boards interlock to keep out water.

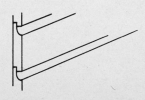

DRY ROT. An erroneous term because wood decays only when moisture is present. A decayed area might be said to have dry rot if the area is now dry, but the "dry" is a superfluous word in that situation.

DRYWALL CONSTRUCTION. A wall or ceiling built of gypsum board. See *gypsum board*.

DUTCHMAN. A piece of wood used to plug any hole or gap, such as a hole made in the wrong place for a plumbing pipe.

E

EBONY. A rare Asian wood prized for inlay work. Some ebony is deep, solid black; other is hazel brown and striped with black. All varieties are hard, heavy and durable.

EDGING. A strip of wood or flexible wood tape used to conceal the edge grain of plywood or to prevent damage to the veneer on a table top, bureau top, etc.

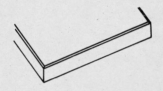

ELASTIC PUTTY. See *putty.*

ELBOW CATCH. See *latch.*

ELEVATION. Plan showing the vertical surfaces of a building as opposed to a floor plan which, in effect, looks down on the building.

ELM. The hard, light-gray-brown, highly figured wood of the American and rock elms is used to a limited extent in furniture. Wood from the burls of the Carparthian elm is considered particularly choice. All elm is hard to work but easy to bend.

EMERY CLOTH. A sandpaper-like material made of cloth coated with a fine, blue-black abrasive stone called emery. It is used primarily on metal, but because of its flexibility it is also used to smooth wood turnings.

EMERY WHEEL. A sharpening, grinding or polishing wheel made of emery.

END-MATCHED. Boards with tongue and groove joints at the ends as well as on the edges. Flooring boards are usually end-matched.

EPOXY GLUE. See *glue.*

ESCUTCHEON. The metal plate surrounding a keyhole. Also the metal plate under a doorknob and covering the opening in the door. Also the metal plates under some types of drawer pulls.

ESSEX BOARD MEASURE. A table of figures on the back of the blade of a framing square that shows at a glance the number of board feet in a board of given dimensions.

EUCALYPTUS. There are many species of eucalyptus and their wood varies considerably. In Australia it is commonly used in heavy construction and is particularly valuable for pilings and other uses in water. However, one species, called Tasmanian oak, has dense, hard, tan wood resembling both oak and ash. This is used to some extent in solid furniture.

EXPANSIVE BIT. See *bit.*

EXTENSION STICK. See *rule.*

F

FACTORY LUMBER. See *lumber*.

FEATHER. A small, thin piece of wood sometimes used in miter joints. See *joint*. As a verb, feather means to work a material to a very thin (feather) edge.

FENCE. An adjustable guide bar on a tool. For example, the steel bar that guides a board through a table saw is a fence. Similarly, a handmade wood fence placed across the corner of a framing square helps in setting a bevel at different angles.

FERRULE. A ring of metal used at the end of a wooden handle on some tools, such as chisels and screwdrivers, to strengthen the handle at the point where the blade enters it. Also a ring of metal fitted over the ends of chair and table legs. Also the metal band holding the bristles in a paint brush.

FIGURE. The wavy grain, mottling or streaking in wood. Bird's-eye maple, for example, has a pronounced figure whereas basswood has none at all.

FILE. Straight, narrow steel tool for taking down wood and metal. Carpenters and woodworkers use files to smooth wood and shape it to a limited extent, and to sharpen other cutting tools.

Files come in 4- to 14-in. lengths without handles; but they should usually be used with handles. They are longitudinally tapered. In profile they are flat, half-round, round, triangular or square.

On single-cut files the teeth are arranged diagonally in parallel lines. On double-cut files, there are two crossing sets of diagonal lines. The coarseness of the teeth gives each file its name. The coarsest type is known as coarse; then come, in order, bastard, second and smooth.

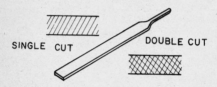

SINGLE CUT   DOUBLE CUT

FILE CLEANER. Also called a file card, this is a wire brush for cleaning files.

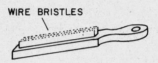

WIRE BRISTLES

FILLER. A paste material that is brushed on oak and other open-pored woods to fill the pores and make for a smoother final finish.

Fillers are also putty and putty-like materials used to fill large holes in wood and other materials.

FILLET. A slender, concave strip of wood inserted for ornamentation between two pieces of wood which meet at an angle.

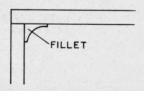

FILLET

FILLISTER. A groove or rabbet. Also a plane used for cutting rabbets.

FINIAL. A carved ornament on the top of a bedpost, breakfront, gable, etc.

FINISHING NAIL. See *nail.*

FINISH LUMBER. See *lumber.*

FIR. The wood of the white fir is almost perfectly white, light in weight, soft and with a uniform, straight grain. It is widely used in construction, although it has only moderate strength and poor resistance to decay.

FIRMER GOUGE. See *gouge.*

FISCHE HINGE. See *hinge.*

FISHED SPLICE. See *splice.*

FISHPLATE. A relatively short board nailed or bolted to the sides of the timbers in a truss to hold them together. It is much like a gusset. Illustrated at *truss.*

FLANGE. A projecting edge. For example, some cabinet doors are rabbeted so that they fit part way into the door opening on the back side but overlap the edges of the opening on the front side. The overlapping piece, commonly known as a lip, is in fact, a flange.

FLANGE

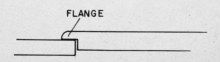

FLAT CORNER BRACE. See *angle iron.*

FLAT POWER BIT. See *bit.*

FLAT SQUARE. See *square.*

FLAT T PLATE. See *mending plate.*

FLINT PAPER. See *sandpaper.*

FLITCH. A log that has been sawed flat on two or four sides and is ready for further processing (although it can be used as is as a rough timber). A flitch is sometimes called a cant.

FLOORING. The most popular woods for flooring are, in order, red oak, white oak and maple. Other woods which are reasonably common (actually, flooring can be made out of any wood) include beech, birch, hickory, pecan, walnut, cherry and yellow pine.

Strip flooring is normally 25/32 in. thick but is produced in other thicknesses. Common widths are 1-1/2, 2, 2-1/4, and 3-1/4 in. The 2-1/4 in. size is most popular. The flooring is usually supplied in random lengths. The boards are tongued and grooved on the sides and ends. Installation is made with cut flooring nails or screw nails.

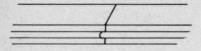

Herringbone flooring consists of short pieces of strip flooring laid in herringbone pattern.

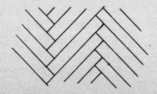

Plank flooring boards range in width from 3 to 10 in. and are installed with screws driven through the face of the boards and covered with plugs. Most plank floors are made of random-width boards.

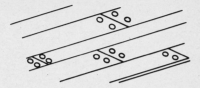

Block flooring and *parquet flooring* are squares available in several sizes. Blocks are made like plywood with three to five horizontal laminations. Parquet blocks are made of strips glued together at the sides. Both materials are today usually laid in mastic.

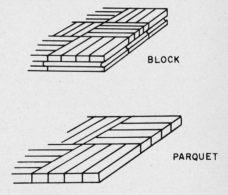

BLOCK

PARQUET

FLUSH. Forming a smooth, level surface. One piece of lumber is said to be flush with another when they are in the same plane.

FLUSH DOOR. In cabinetwork, a flush door is one which is set into the cabinet frame so that, when closed, door and frame form a smooth surface. In the building industry, a flush door is a slab door with a smooth, unbroken surface.

FLUTE. A fairly large, rounded groove used to decorate columns and the trim around doors and fireplaces. Such pieces are said to be fluted.

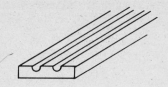

FLUTER. See *gouge.*

FOERSTNER BIT. See *bit.*

FOLDING RULE. See *rule.*

FOOT BOLT. See *bolt, locking.*

FORE PLANE. See *plane.*

FRAME. To erect the framework or superstructure of a building. This consists of assembling numerous large timbers such as joists, studs, rafters, girders, etc.

FRAMING SQUARE. See *square.*

FRETWORK. An ornamental work of interlacing, angular lines. Often denotes work with a perforated design made by frequent piercing to form a screen.

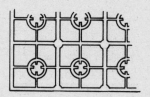

FRICTION CATCH. See *catch.*

FRIEZE. The exposed horizontal member just below the cornice of a building or furniture piece.

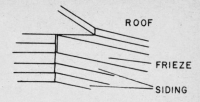

FUR. To apply narrow boards, called furring strips, to a surface in order to provide a nailing base for a covering material. For example, when paneling a basement playroom, furring strips are attached to the foundation walls and the paneling is then nailed to them. The principal purpose in this instance is to provide an air space between the possibly damp concrete and the paneling. The process followed is called "furring out the wall."

   Similarly, if a ceiling is badly cracked and irregular, you might "fur it down" by nailing furring strips to it and then nailing gypsum board panels to the strips.

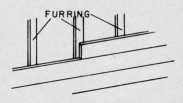

G

GABOON. Also called Samara. A straight-grained, red-dish-brown African wood used in paneling and furniture. It is fairly strong and light.

GAIN. The mortise or notch cut in a piece of lumber to receive the end of a second piece.

GARNET PAPER. See *sandpaper*.

GATE LATCH. See *latch*.

GAUGE. Depending on their design, gauges are used for making or controlling measurements and marking work to be done on lumber and plywood.

Marking gauge is a rule-like device with a sharp pin at one end of a wooden or metal beam (bar) and a head that can be slid up and down the beam. The tool is used for marking lines parallel with the planed edge of a board or timber. The head is set the desired distance from the pin. The beam is then laid flat on the board with the head snug against one edge, and the gauge is moved the length of the board. The pin scratches a line into the board.

Butt gauge is a somewhat similar tool for marking the position and thickness of hinge butts on doors and jambs. It can also be used to mark the location of strikeplates, lock plates, etc.

Depth gauge measures the depth of a hole. The simplest type of gauge consists of a body which is placed flat on the surface into which the hole is drilled. A scale is then pushed down through the body to the bottom of the hole.

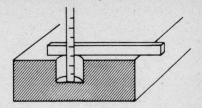

Bit gauge controls the depth to which a hole is drilled. It is clamped to the shank of an auger bit and revolves with the bit. The hole is drilled to the proper depth when the bottom of the gauge strikes the wood surface around the hole.

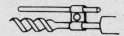

Drill stop is comparable to a bit gauge but is used on twist drills under 1/2 in. diameter. It is a fat, round collar that is fitted over the drill and adjusted to the desired drilling depth.

BIT

GIMLET. A T-shaped tool consisting of a small drill and a wooden handle for boring holes. It is a miniature auger.

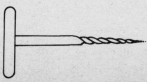

GIRDER. A heavy wood or steel beam used to support joists in the middle of a building which is too wide for the joists to span alone.

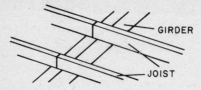

A spaced girder is made of joist timbers with a space between them. It is used when pipes or heating ducts must be run through the girder.

GIRTH. The circumference of a round timber, table, etc.

GLIDE. A small, stainless steel dome fastened to the bottom of a furniture leg to facilitate sliding.

GLUE. Adhesives for bonding wood to wood, or wood to another material such as metal or felt, are almost too numerous to count. Unhappily, they are often identified only by trade names and not by descriptive generic names. The glues most often used by woodworkers and carpenters are the following:

Animal glue made from hides and other animal parts is sold in sheet, flake or powder form which must be heated before use. It is also available as a liquid that is applied cold. The glue is strong but has poor resistance to moisture and becomes brittle with age.

Casein glue made from milk curd is a powder to which water is added. It is water-resistant but not waterproof.

Contact cement is a viscous liquid that forms a tight bond without clamping. It is used mainly for sticking plastic laminates to plywood or particleboard.

Epoxy glue is an extremely strong, moisture-resistant glue. It is especially useful when you need a sound joint between two small wood surfaces and when you are bonding wood to some other material such as metal, leather or pottery. Most epoxy glues come in two tubes which are combined immediately before using.

Plastic-resin glue is made in powder form from urea-formaldehyde. It is mixed with water for use. Although water-resistant, it is not recommended for outdoor use. And it should not be used for joints that are not well fitted.

Polyvinyl-resin glue is a white liquid, colorless when dry. It is easy to use but only moderately strong and lacks moisture resistance.

Resorcinol glue is a two-part adhesive made by mixing a red liquid with a powder. It is the best glue for outdoor uses and is very strong. It leaves a dark red stain, however.

GLUE GUN. An electric tool for melting and applying a synthetic glue and a sealing compound, both of which come in stick form. The glue is used for joining wood and other materials; the sealer for caulking boats, gutters, etc.

GONCALO ALVES. A hard, difficult-to-work, South American furniture wood. It is reddish-brown woven through with black streaks.

GOUGE. Chisel-like cutting tool with rounded or V-shaped cutting edge. Gouges are used for digging out wood and making grooves. They are manipulated either by hand or with the aid of a mallet or soft-face hammer.

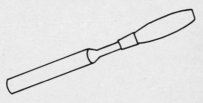

Carpenters' gouges have blades with parallel edges. They are classified either as firmer gouges or paring gouges and both are available with flat, medium or regular sweeps (curves). Widths range from 1/8 to 2 in.

Firmer gouges, made with the bevel of the cutting edge ground on the outside, are the type used for most work. Paring gouges, which are ground on the inside, are used to cut deep, straight curved openings and light concave outlines with the grain.

Woodcarvers' gouges are made in widths of from 1/32 to 1 in. The largest sizes have tapering blades and are known as fishtail gouges. The smaller sizes with straight blades with parallel sides are called straight gouges. Gouges which are slightly bent at the tip so they can be used for deep work are called bent gouges. Those in which the entire shank is curved to form a very loose letter S are called spades.

Like woodcarvers' chisels, woodcarvers' gouges are numbered to indicate the shape of the cutting edge and depth of cut. (The numbers have nothing to do with blade widths.) Nos. 3 to 9 have sweeps shaped like an arc; No. 9, the deepest, forms a semi-circle; No. 10 has a U-shaped cutting edge and is known as a fluter; No. 11 forms a slightly deeper U and is known as a veiner; Nos. 39 to 41 are V shaped and called parting tools or V tools. All these gouges fall into either the straight or fishtail categories.

Nos. 21 to 32 have arc-shaped cutting edges of increasing depth; Nos. 43 and 44 are parting tools. These chisels have bent shanks.

Gouges for *wood turning* are similar to carpenters' gouges, but have short blades and very long handles.

GRAIN. The direction in which the fibers in a piece of wood run. In straight-grained wood, the fibers lie in more or less straight lines parallel to the edges of the piece. In cross-grained wood, the fibers are at an angle to the edges. And in wood with a spiral grain, the fibers follow a spiral pattern around the wood.

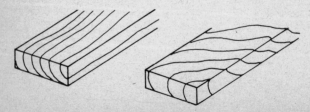

Wood is said to be fine-grained if it has small cells and a resulting dense, smooth texture. It is said to be close-grained if the growth rings are narrow. By contrast, a coarse-grained or open-grained wood has wide growth rings and/or large, open cells resulting in a somewhat porous, rough texture.

End-grain is the grain exposed when a piece of wood is cut cross-wise. This is called "cutting across the grain" as opposed to "working with the grain."

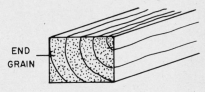

END GRAIN

Edge-grain and *vertical-grain* are interchangeable terms used to describe softwood lumber sawed so that the growth rings form an angle of 45° or more with the wide faces of the lumber. In other words, if you examine an end of the board, you will see that the growth rings cross it at a sharp angle. On the face of the board, the grain is close and uniform, as if it had been cut into the board with a comb.

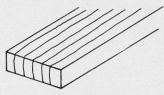

Flat-grain is a term describing softwood lumber sawed so that the growth rings form an angle of less than 45° with the wide faces of the lumber. In such a piece of wood, the spacing between the growth rings on the face is variable.

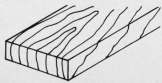

Mixed-grain lumber contains both edge-grain and flat-grain.

The comparable terms describing hardwood lumber are *quarter-sawed, plain-sawed* and *bastard-sawed*.

Flat-grain and plain-sawed lumber is more common and cheaper than edge-grain and quarter-sawed lumber, and knots affect its strength and appearance less. But edge-grain and quarter-sawed lumber shrinks and warps less, is less likely to split, and wears more evenly.

GREEN WOOD. Unseasoned wood. The lumber industry today considers any wood having more than 19% moisture content to be green wood, even though it may have been seasoned. Because green wood is not as strong as seasoned wood, the actual dimensions of lumber cut from it are slightly greater than the dimensions of seasoned (dry) lumber.

GRINDER. This is the modern-day grindstone, so named because the revolving wheels now used for sharpening tools are made, not of natural stone, but of abrasive materials pressed and baked in a furnace.

The simplest grinder is turned by a handcrank; but since accurate grinding requires that you hold the tool you are sharpening in two hands, you need a helper to turn the grinder. This is probably the main reason why the majority of grinders now in use are electric machines mounted on a bench. These generally come with two grinding wheels, although in some cases one is a buffing wheel. Wheel diameters range from 5-1/2 to 10 in. Most machines operate in the vicinity of 3000 rpm, but those with large wheels are considerably slower.

GRINDER, ROTARY. A small, electric hand tool used mainly by hobbyists for carving, cutting, drilling and sanding wood, plastic and soft metals. Also called a hand shaper.

GROUND. A rough, narrow board nailed flush with the surface of a plaster wall. The baseboard and other trim are then nailed to it.

GROWTH RING. The growth rings of wood are visible in a stump, log butt or end grain of a piece of lumber. Each ring represents a year's growth. In addition to revealing the age of trees, growth rings indicate the strength of the wood. The narrower the rings are, the stronger the wood is. The strength of the wood is further increased if the growth rings contain a high percentage of summerwood.

Wood showing narrow growth rings is said to be close-grained. That with a goodly amount of summerwood is dense. Woods that are both close-grained and dense are usually especially good for structural work.

GUM. A hardwood of moderate weight and hardness much used in furniture-making. The sapwood is pinkish-white; the heartwood, reddish-brown. The grain is normally rather inconspicuous but the wood is occasionally highly figured and valued for paneling.

The wood known as gum comes from the sweet gum tree. The wood of the sour gum tree and of some eucalyptus trees is occasionally called gum but is described here under *tupelo* and *eucalyptus*.

GUSSET. A small board or piece of plywood which strengthens a corner in a truss or comparable piece of work. When trusses are mass-produced in factories, steel gussets with numerous nail-like projections are often used to speed the assembly process. Illustrated at *truss*.

GYPSUM BOARD. Interior wall and ceiling panels made of gypsum plaster covered on both sides with strong paper. These are widely used in light construction today in place of plaster. The panels are 4 ft. wide; 8 ft. long; and 3/8, 1/2 or 5/8 in. thick. After the panels are nailed to studs or joists, the joints between them are usually concealed with a paper tape embedded in and covered with about three coats of a special cement.

In most construction today, gypsum board is installed by crews of sheetrockers and the joints are completed by tapers. But carpenters and handymen make installations, too.

H

HACKBERRY. A heavy yellowish hardwood with a strong figure, sometimes used in furniture.

HACKSAW. See *saw, hand*.

HAFT. The handle of a cutting or thrusting tool, such as a knife or chisel.

HALF-ROUND. A molding shaped like half of a circle and used to cover joints between panels or boards in the same plane. Widths range from 3/8 to 1-3/4 in.

HALVED SPLICE. See *splice*.

HAMMER. The standard hammer used by people working with wood has a head with a more or less flat, round striking face at one end and a claw for pulling nails at the other. But many tools fitting this description that are called hammers are very inefficient items.

Good hammers with hardwood, fiberglass or steel handles average about 13 in. long, generally weigh 16 or 20 oz., and are balanced so they swing easily.

Reasonably close examination will reveal that the striking face varies. On some hammers it is slightly convex to allow you to drive a nail flush with the surface without denting it. Furthermore, you can hit the nail with a somewhat slanting blow without making a dent in the surface. This kind of hammer is said to be bell-faced.

By contrast, a plain-faced hammer has a flat striking surface; and for this reason may be used only for rough work. In some cases, flat hammer faces are criss-crossed with shallow lines so they won't skid off a nail head. These are called checker-faced.

FLAT FACE   BELL FACE   CHECKED FACE

The claws on hammers are either curved or straight. The former are better for pulling nails; the latter, for ripping boards apart.

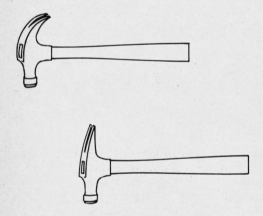

Two slight variations of the standard carpenter's hammer are the heavy-duty hammer and floor-layer's hammer. The heavy-duty model is 3 in. longer than average, has a ripping claw and an extra-big face. The floor-layer's hammer has a short handle, weighs 2 lb. and has an extra-big octagonal face.

The only other hammer commonly used in woodworking is a soft-face hammer with a small, mallet-like head. This has two faces, both made of plastic. It can be used instead of a mallet when you are working with a chisel.

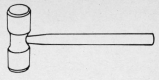

HAND DRILL. See *drill*.

HAND SCRAPER. See *scraper*.

HAND SCREW. A large clamp. See *clamp*.

HAND SHAPER, ELECTRIC. See *grinder, rotary*.

HANGER. A stirrup-like steel strap that is attached to a beam or joist to support the end of another beam or joist at the same level. Also called a stirrup.

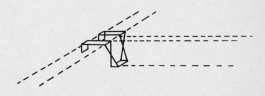

HARDBOARD. A very hard, dense, strong, durable sheet material made of compressed wood fibers. Most commonly sold in 4-by 8-ft. panels of 1/8 or 1/4-in. thickness, it is used for interior parts of furniture, cabinets, soffits, wall and ceiling paneling, siding, work surfaces, etc.

The standard hardboard is brown in color, and is smooth on the front side and slightly textured on the back side. Other hardboards come with a tough baked-enamel finish in various colors on the front side. Still others are embossed on the front side.

Although all types of hardboard have considerable resistance to moisture, only tempered hardboard should be used outdoors or in damp locations indoors.

HARDWARE. The vast assortment of metal parts that go into a building, cabinet or furniture piece. (But it does not include all of them because some things, such as towel rods and soap dishes in bathrooms, are called fittings.)

In a building, the hidden hardware items, such as the nails and hangers, are called rough hardware; the exposed items, such as the locks and window catches, are finish hardware.

Hardware is also categorized as builder's hardware (this includes locksets, latchsets, hinges, door stops, door closers, window locks, etc.); cabinet hardware (including catches, pulls, knobs and hinges used in cabinets and furniture); and drapery hardware (curtain rods, tiebacks, etc.).

HARDWOOD. A misleading term used to differentiate broad-leaved trees, such as oaks and magnolias, and the lumber they yield, from softwood trees and lumber. In actual fact, most hardwoods are harder than softwoods, but several softwoods are harder than several hardwoods.

HASP. A locking device used on chests, doors, etc. The most common design is a hinged metal strap with a slot that fits over a staple and is then held secure by a padlock or peg slipped through the staple. In another design, closely resembling the ordinary hook and eye, the hasp is a hook that slips over the staple.

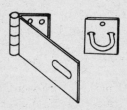

HATCHET. A short-handled axe usually with a hammer head and a slot in the blade for pulling nails. The cutting edge of the more or less triangular blade is straight. Hatchets are used mainly for laying wood floors and wood shingle and shake roofs and for rough-cutting and pointing boards and timbers.

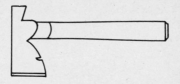

HEADER. A large timber to which joists are attached at right angles when framing around an opening in a floor or roof. Most headers are made by nailing together two pieces of joist lumber, but a single 4-in.-thick timber may be used.

The heavy horizontal timber over a door or window opening is also called a header, but is properly known as a *lintel*.

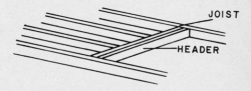

HEART SHAKE. A split across the very center, or heart, of a log. The split runs across the growth rings and is wider at the heart than near the circumference of the log. There may be only a single split or several splits running in different directions. Compare *check*.

HEARTWOOD. The mature, inner wood in a tree trunk or large limb. It is usually darker in color than the sapwood, which forms a ring around it. In most characteristics there is little or no difference between heartwood and sapwood; but the former is, in some woods such as oak, more resistant to decay.

HELVE. The handle of a hammer, mallet, hatchet or axe.

HEMLOCK. A reddish-colored softwood with no outstanding characteristics and no outstanding defects. Easily worked, it is much used in construction.

HERRINGBONE FLOORING. See *flooring.*

HICKORY. A hard, heavy, resilient hardwood used for handles of tools, bats and other purposes where great strength is called for. It is light brown.

HINGE. Hinge selection is dictated by the size and weight of the door, by the desired appearance of the door when hung, by the location of the door and the way it will be used, and by the amount of work you are willing to do to install the hinges. Choice is complicated by the availability of so many different types in so many different metals and finishes.

Butt hinges are the most widely used, especially in building. They are square or rectangular but are not necessarily flat when open. If the leaves have been swaged, they lie parallel when closed and there is little space between them. If the leaves have not been swaged, the space between them when closed is wedge-shaped and it becomes necessary to increase the depth of the mortises in order to avoid a wide crack between the door and jamb.

Large butt hinges generally have a loose pin in the knuckles (the barrel-like loops on the leaves) to make it easier to take a heavy door down and put it up. Smaller hinges generally have a fixed pin. An intermediate type of hinge is called a *loose-joint hinge*. The leaf at the

bottom has a fixed pin; the top leaf is slipped down over
this. Loose-joint hinges are made in right-hand and left-
hand models to ensure that the leaf with the pin is always at the bottom.

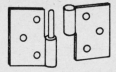

In situations where complete mortising is impossible,
a *half-mortised* or *half-surface butt hinge* is used. With
the former, the door leaf is mortised and the jamb leaf,
which is approximately half the width of the door leaf,
is applied to the surface of the jamb. With a half-surface
hinge, on the other hand, the jamb leaf is mortised and
the half-size door leaf is applied to the door surface.

A *parliament hinge* is akin to a conventional butt
hinge but is much wider and has an H shape. It is used
on building doors when it is necessary to provide clear-
ance between a door and the jamb casing or adjacent
wall when the door is thrown open. A *wide-throw hinge*
serves the same purpose but is rectangular.

Non-mortise hinges have leaves with three straps
which interlock when the door is closed; thus, even
though they are screwed to the surface of the jamb and
door edge, there is only a small crack between the surfaces. The pins are loose.

Building hinges with small, decorative knuckles are named *olive knuckle, paumelle* and *fische.* All are loose-joint hinges. The leaves are mortised into the door edge and jamb.

Strap hinges with fixed pins are surface-mounted; used when appearances are unimportant and when the door is so wide and heavy that an edge-attached hinge would not support it.

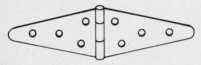

T hinges are also fixed-pin utility hinges, usually used on large doors. The rectangular leaf is mortised into the jamb; the strap leaf is surface-mounted.

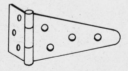

H and H-L hinges, so named because of their shape, are surface-mounted on cabinets. They have fixed pins and usually a rustic hammered finish.

Cabinet hinges, semi-concealed and fixed pin type, are of different designs for different styles of door. In some cases, the slender jamb leaf is exposed; in other cases, only the pin is exposed. The door leaf folds around and is attached to the edge and back of the door. The same kind of hinge must be used on large plywood doors, because screws do not hold well in the edges of plywood.

Complete concealment of hinges is achieved in doors with the *invisible hinge,* which is mortised into the door edge and jamb. But most concealed hinges on cabinet doors are *pivot hinges.* These are much less expensive and are surface-mounted. If you look hard, however, you can see the pivots when the door is closed.

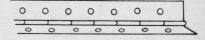

Piano hinges are very long, narrow hinges used for heavy table leaves, piano tops, etc. *Drop-leaf hinges,* by contrast, are very short, wide hinges used on drop-leaf tables. *Back-flap hinges* are similar but a little wider.

Double-acting hinges are used on folding screens so you can open them in either direction.

Other specialized hinges are the *double-acting* type for use on heavy swinging doors; the *pivot* for light swinging doors and floor-to-ceiling doors; *Swing-Clear hinges* designed specifically for hospitals but useful wherever a completely clear door opening is desired; *spring hinges* for use on cabinet doors; and *screw-hook-and-strap* hinges for hanging shutters.

HIP RAFTER. See *rafter.*

H-L HINGE. See *hinge.*

HOLE SAW. See *saw, hand.*

HOLLOW-WALL SCREW ANCHOR. See *molly screw.*

HOLLY. A creamy-white wood used in inlay work. It is hard and has almost no visible grain.

HONDURAS MAHOGANY. Not a true mahogany; nevertheless, it is a rich, golden to reddish-brown, fine-textured wood with scattered pores. It is often highly figured, though it generally has a straight, uniform grain. Easily worked, strong and durable, it is used in furniture and paneling.

HONEYCOMB. Small white pockets in wood caused by a fungus. They do not weaken the wood.

HOOK AND EYE. A simple latching device used on doors and out-swinging windows. Because the hook moves in a hemisphere, it does not have to be mounted in the same plane as the eye. For example, the hook can be mounted on a door and the eye mounted several inches forward of it on the door jamb.

HOPPER JOINT. See *joint.*

HORSE. A trestle-like or stool-like wooden structure used as a temporary support during a construction project.

HOUSED STRINGER. A stair stringer with horizontal and vertical grooves cut in the side to receive the ends of the treads and risers. A housed stringer is stronger than a cutout stringer with a saw-tooth edge.

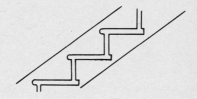

I

IMBUYA. A rich brown, fine-textured, rather heavy hardwood from Brazil. It is used in furniture, paneling and flooring.

INCENSE CEDAR. A light-weight, non-resinous, reddish-brown softwood with a uniform, fine texture. Like other cedars, it has a pleasant aroma and the heartwood is highly resistant to decay. It is used in construction.

INLAY. To set small pieces of wood, marble, glass, etc. into a surface, usually of wood, for decorative purposes. The design thus created is also called an inlay, or inlaid work.

INSHAVE. A U-shaped cutting tool for hollowing out bowls, chair seats and the like. The crosspiece of the U is the blade; the uprights, the handles.

INSIDE CORNER. A corner which forms an angle of less than 180°, such as the corner of a room. It is also called an internal corner and is the opposite of an external or outside corner.

INSIDE CORNER

INSIDE-START SAW. See *saw, hand.*

INTAGLIO. A carving which is sunk below the surface.

INTERNAL CORNER. See *inside corner*.

INVISIBLE HINGE. See *hinge*.

IROKO. Also called African teak; a fine-textured, rich brown wood with zigzag yellow bands. It is used in furniture and paneling and, in Africa, for bowls and carving.

J

JACK KNIFE. See *pocket knife.*

JACK PLANE. See *plane.*

JACK POST. A steel post with a jack in the upper end used to raise sagging floors or support floors which are heavily loaded. The jack has screw threads and is raised by turning. Short posts will extend to 3 ft.; long posts, to almost 8 ft.

JACK RAFTER. See *rafter.*

JACK SCREW. A jack essentially similar to a jack post but smaller. The smallest size extends to only about 12 in.; the largest, to 24 in.

JAMB. One of the inner surfaces of door and window openings. In a door opening the strikeplate for the lock is set in one side jamb; the hinges are set into the other side jamb. The jamb at the top of the opening is called the head jamb.

In a window opening, the jambs include the stops, stiles and parting strips.

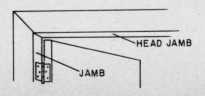

JIG SAW. See *saw, hand* and *saw, shop.*

JOINERY. A woodworker's name for the various joints he uses.

JOINTER. An electrically driven shop tool with a long, flat steel work table with a horizontal revolving cutter 4 to 12 in. wide recessed in the center. The tool is used for planing, rabbeting, tapering, beveling, chamfering and molding lumber, and for making warped boards flat. It is also known as a jointer-planer.

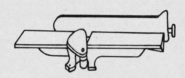

JOINTS. Next to sawing lumber straight, the most important job in carpentry and woodworking is knowing how to put pieces together neatly and securely. Fortunately, there are many ways of doing this.

Butt joints are the simplest joints—and also the weakest. The end of the piece which is being butted must be cut square. The two pieces are then held together with nails, screws, dowels, glue, corrugated or other special fasteners, mending plates or wood blocks. The various possibilities are illustrated. (For butting boards and timbers end to end, see *splice.*)

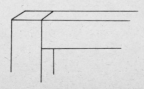

Rabbet joints are used to join boards side to side or to form a corner. In the latter case, a rabbet is cut in the end of one piece; and the squared end of the other piece is set into this. In edge-joining, the usual practice is to cut corresponding rabbets in both boards and to fit one into the other in the manner of shiplap. The less

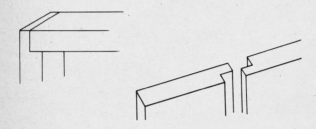

common alternative is to butt the rabbeted edges together to form a groove, and to fasten them with a glued spline.

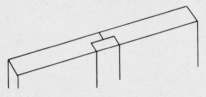

In *dado joints,* a groove is cut across a board (but not at the very end) and the second board is fitted into this. In a *housed dado joint*, the entire end of the second board is inserted in the dado. In a *stopped dado joint*, the dado is cut only part way across the first board and the second board is notched at the end.

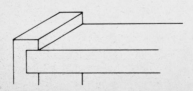

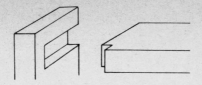

The *shoulder-housed dado joint* is also called rabbet and dado, and is used to form corners as illustrated. The *dovetail dado joint* is shaped in profile like a half dovetail, and the second piece is notched to fit.

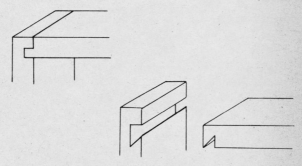

Tongue and groove joints—also known as a matched joints—join boards along their edges.

Mortise and tenon joints are widely used by furniture and cabinet makers. A mortise is cut in one piece; a tongue-like tenon corresponding to the mortise is shaped in the end of the second piece. The tenon is normally glued into the mortise; although for maximum strength it is sometimes secured with a wood pin driven through the sides of the mortise and the tenon.

A *stub mortise and tenon joint* is a blind joint with a very short tenon inserted into a mortise in the face of a board.

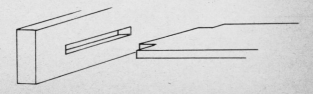

Miter joints are a type of butt joint in which the pieces to be joined are mitered to corresponding angles and then fitted together. The resulting joints are a little stronger than an ordinary butt joint and more attractive.

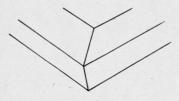

The usual way of fastening a miter joint is with nails alone, nails and glue, or special fasteners. Dowels are often used.

Tongued miter joints have the mitered edges tongued and grooved and then glued. In a *splined miter joint,* both edges are grooved and held together with a glued spline. A *slip-feather miter joint* is similar except that the wood insert is thinner. In another type of slip-feather joint, the groove is cut across the arris, and a triangular feather is inserted.

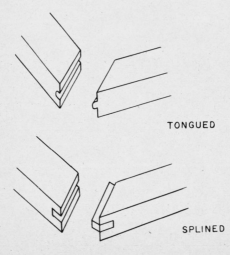

TONGUED

SPLINED

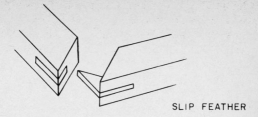

SLIP FEATHER

Hopper joints are the corner joints in a four-sided pyramid or slant-sided hopper. They require a butt joint of over 90° and a miter cut of over 45°. A framing square is required to figure out the joint.

Coped joints are butt joints made in moldings, at the inside corners of rooms. The end of one molding is cut with a coping saw to fit snugly against the contoured side of the second molding.

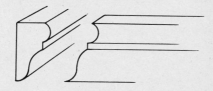

Lap joints can be made by nailing, screwing or bolting one board to the surface of another board, but the joints are weak and ugly. *Half-lap joints* are superior in every way. In these, identical notches to half the depth of the wood are made in the pieces to be joined. The pieces are then fitted together and secured with nails, screws and/or glue.

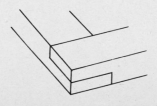

In a *through mortise and tenon joint*, the mortise is cut all the way through the wood and the end of the tenon is visible. On the other hand, in a *blind mortise and tenon joint*, the mortise is cut only part way into the wood and the tenon is completely concealed.

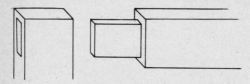

A *haunched mortise and tenon joint* is used in the corner of a panel door. The haunch, which is a cut-back part of the tenon, fills the end of the groove cut in the stile to receive the panels.

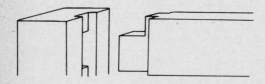

A *mitered mortise and tenon joint* is used when a piece of wood, such as a chair leg, is mortised on two sides. The ends of both tenons are mitered so they fit together in the mortise. The *cross-lap mortise and tenon joint* has a similar purpose.

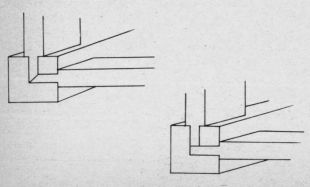

A *keyed mortise and tenon joint* is a through joint in which the tenon protrudes some distance out of the mortise. The protruding part, in turn, is mortised to receive a wood wedge called a key.

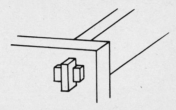

Wedged and *foxtailed mortise and tenon joints* are designed for maximum resistance to loosening. In the wedged joint, the through mortise is slightly flared at top and bottom; and after the tenon is inserted, thin wedges are driven into the cracks. In some cases, wedges are also driven into saw kerfs made in the end of the tenon.

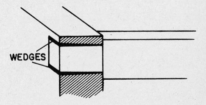

A *foxtailed joint* is a blind joint. Two saw kerfs are made across the end of the tenon, and wedges are inserted. As the tenon is driven into the mortise, the wedges are forced into the kerfs, thus binding the tenon against the mortise at top and bottom.

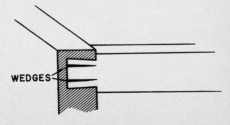

An *open mortise and tenon joint*, or slip joint, is used at corners of window screen frames, and similar articles. The mortise is notched into the end of one piece; the tenon is cut in the end of the other piece; and the two are slipped together much as a letter goes into an envelope.

Dovetail joints are used in building drawers and frames for furniture and cabinets in which you need maximum strength. The joints have interlocking teeth which are very difficult to cut without a router.

A *half-lap dovetail joint* is used to tie the end of one piece into the side of another. A *single dovetail joint* is a corner joint used to unite narrow boards. A *multiple dovetail joint* is a series of single dovetails.

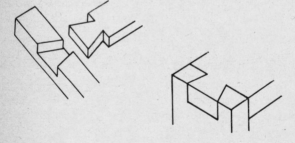

Other types of joint are called the *stopped lap dovetail*; the *lap*, or *half-blind*, *dovetail*; and the *secret*, or *blind*, *dovetail*.

JOIST. A large horizontal timber used to support a floor or roof with very little slope and to which a ceiling is nailed. Joists may be designated as floor joists, roof joists or ceiling joists, depending on their main function; but some joists, of course, have two functions. In a two-story house, for instance, the first story ceiling is attached to the same joists which support the second-story floor.

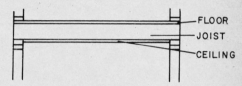

Joists generally have a nominal thickness of 2 in. but may be as much as 4 in. thick. In width they range upwards from 6 in. If a joist is supported only at the ends, its span is limited by its size, how it is graded, the type of wood from which it is made, the load it must support and the spacing between the joists. For example, a top-grade 2 x 8 Douglas fir floor joist can be used to span a 14-ft. space if the spacing between joists is 16 in. and the live load supported by the floor is 30 lb. per square ft. But if you use a comparable 2 x 10 joist, you can span 17 ft. By contrast, if the joists are made of white fir, the allowable span for a 2 x 8 is only 12-1/2 ft. and for a 2 x 10, 15-1/2 ft.

JUNIOR-JACK PLANE. See *plane*.

K

KELOBRA. A hardwood from Central America which goes into furniture. It is greenish-brown, has a large, wavy figure and a coarse texture.

KERF. A saw cut. Because saw teeth are bent slightly to the sides, the kerf is wider than the thickness of the blade.

KEY. A small piece of wood which is set into a larger piece much as a key slips into a lock. Keys are used in keyed mortise and tenon joints. See *joint*. They are also set into boards across the grain to prevent warping.

As a verb, key means to roughen a surface so that something which is then applied will stick better.

KEYHOLE SAW. See *saw, hand*.

KILN-DRIED LUMBER. Lumber dried in an oven. See *air-dried lumber*.

KING POST The vertical timber in the center of a truss. Many trusses, however, are made without king posts.

KNEE. A timber bent or sawed like a knee which is used to relieve the strain on another timber.

KNIFE. See *pocket knife*.

KNOTS. Knots in lumber are the remnants of branches covered over by the tree trunk as it grew. They are classified as defects because they detract from the appearance of lumber and reduce its strength if it is put under tension or used as a beam. This does not mean, however, that lumber containing knots is unsafe to use in many situations.

Knots are classified as pin knots if less than 1/2 in. across; small knots if between 1/2 and 3/4 in.; medium knots if between 3/4 and 1-1/2 in.; and large knots if more than 1-1/2 in.

A loose knot is one which is not firmly held by the surrounding wood. If it falls out, it leaves a knot hole. A tight knot is the exact opposite. It is so firmly fixed in the wood that nothing can move it. In between these two extremes is the fixed knot, which can normally be expected to hold but which can be loosened under pressure.

As opposed to the average knot, which is more or less round, a spike knot is a long oval or elliptical knot resulting from the fact that the saw cut through the branch stub lengthwise.

KOA. A hard, red or golden-brown furniture and paneling wood from the Hawaiian Islands. Some of it has a beautiful fiddle-back figure. In straight-grained pieces, there are black stripes.

KORINA. See *limba.*

L

LACEWOOD. A coarse-grained, reddish wood with prominent medullary rays from the Australian silk oak. When the wood is quarter-sawed, the medullary rays have a uniform flakey figure suggestive of lace. Lacewood is used in furniture, and in Australia it is also used for interior trim.

LALLY COLUMN. A vertical steel pipe filled with concrete. It is used to support long girders at or near their centers.

LAMINATE. To glue together layers or plies of wood or other material. The laminating process is no different from the veneering process. However, there seems to be a general assumption that in laminated construction there are at least three plies, while in veneer there are only two plies, one thick and one thin.

The most familiar laminated product is plywood. But with the advent of modern glues, the construction industry has shown more and more interest in huge laminated beams and trusses. These can be shaped in almost any way; have great strength; and are handsome enough to be left exposed.

LAP JOINT. See *joint.*

LARCH. A heavy, hard, strong softwood with an exceptionally straight, fine, uniform grain. The sapwood is yellowish and usually removed before the log is cut into boards. The heartwood is uniformly reddish-brown. The wood is used in construction.

LATCH. Device for closing and holding a door shut until turned or lifted. It has no locking mechanism. Compare *catch.*

The most familiar is the *interior door latch* used on inside doors of houses and other buildings. In older latches, the mechanism is enclosed in a cast-iron box which is mortised into the edge of the door. This type is still made, but most modern latches are tubular units installed by drilling a large hole through the faces of the door and a small hole for the latch tongue in the edge of the door.

A *sliding door latch* is set into the edge of the door and has a slender tongue which hooks on to the strike-plate when the thumb screw is turned. The latch can be operated from both sides of the door.

Screen and storm door latches can also be operated from both sides but the latch mechanism is mounted on the inside. In many cases, levers or pushbuttons are used instead of knobs.

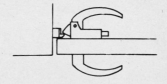

An older type of latch usually made of black iron is a *thumb latch*. The handle has a thumb depresser on one side of the door and an L-shaped lift on the other side.

When the door is closed, pressing the former or lifting the latter raises the latch tongue out of a groove in the strikeplate on the jamb.

LATCH OPEN

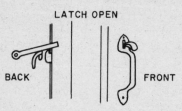

BACK   FRONT

Surface latches are used on small doors that are opened only from the pull side. In the oldest type, the latch tongue is loosely screwed to the door or to a metal plate which is screwed to the door, and is raised and lowered (parallel with the door) by hand. It engages a groove in the strikeplate on the door trim.

A newer kind of surface latch is a bow-shaped handle with a thumb button at the top. This controls the tongue on the reverse side of the door.

Another surface latch is a *gate latch* with a hook that slips over a strike bar mounted on the gate post. The latch closes automatically when it hits the strike. It is opened by a trigger handle on top of the hook.

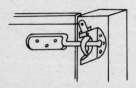

Several types of latch are commonly called catches. One is a *transom catch,* or chain bolt, used for holding clerestory and other high-up windows closed. It is mounted with the tongue in vertical position, and is unlatched by pulling a ring or chain in the bottom of the housing.

An *elbow catch* is used on one of a pair of double cabinet doors. It is installed inside the cabinet and must be released by hand. It consists of a finger-operated hook mounted on the door which engages an L-shaped strikeplate in the top of the cabinet.

A *cupboard catch* is a large door latch mounted on the surface of the door and operable only from that side.

LATEX PUTTY. See *putty.*

LATH. A strip of rough lumber 1-1/2 in. wide, 3/8 in. thick and 4 ft. long which was formerly used as a base for plaster. The steel mesh and sheets of gypsum which are now used as a plaster base are also called lath.

LATHE. The wood lathe is a shop tool used for turning long pieces of wood between the headstock and tailstock spindles and for turning short, wide pieces on a faceplate. Most machines are driven by a separate motor connected with belts; but a few have built-in motors. The speed is variable. Wood chisels and gouges are used to shape the revolving wood.

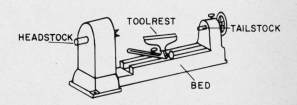

LATTICEWORK. A criss-cross pattern usually made of thin strips of wood, called lattice strips. In some cases, however, latticework is made by cutting out a panel of plywood, hardboard, etc.

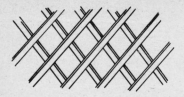

LAUAN. One of the Philippine woods sold as Philippine mahogany.

LAUREL. A brown to gray wood with black streaks and frequently prominent figuring like that in black walnut. Hard and coarse-grained, it is used in furniture. It comes from an Indian tree, not the American plant known as laurel.

LEAD ANCHOR. See *rawl plug*.

LEDGER. A horizontal timber nailed to the face of studs or girders or, in an existing building, to the face of a wall to support floor joists. A ledger is also one of the horizontal supports on which the planks rest in a scaffold.

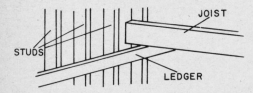

LEVEL. Also called spirit level, this device is used to determine whether a surface is horizontal (level) or vertical (plumb). Depending on the design, it can also be used to determine the angle of a surface.

Levels are slim, rectangular tools ranging from 1 to 6-1/2 ft. long. They are made of wood or metal with small glass or plastic vials set into the body to protect them against breakage. The vials are partly filled with alcohol. An air bubble is centered in the vials when the surface being checked is level or plumb.

The vial which checks horizontal is at the middle of the level and is parallel with the long edges. The vial which checks vertical is at one end of the level and at right angles to the long edges. The vial which checks angles is at the other end of the level (but relatively few levels include this vial). In some cases, the angle vial is used only to determine a $45°$ miter. In other cases, it is used to determine any angle from $0°$ to $90°$.

Line levels are pencil-size devices which are hooked to a cord when you want to establish a level line between widely separated points.

LID SUPPORT. A slotted, flat metal strip used to hold open the lids of chests and lift-top desks and also to prevent them from crashing backward.

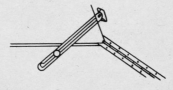

LIGHT FRAMING LUMBER. Lumber used in light construction. It has a nominal thickness and width of 2 to 4 in. The most common size of light framing lumber is the 2 x 4 which is used for studs.

LIGNUM VITAE. A hard, very heavy wood with a prominent grain from Central and South America. It is used for making such things as pulley blocks and also used for carving. It is black to greenish-brown in color.

LIMBA. Also called korina. A yellow to light brown hardwood of fine texture and with straight grain. It is used mainly in paneling and to some extent in modern furniture. It comes from West Africa.

LIME. The name given in Europe primarily to basswood.

LINEAL FOOT. The standard unit of measure for moldings, interior trim, furring strips and grounds, regardless of their width and thickness. In other words, a 1/2 in. quarter-round molding and a base molding 5-1/2 in. wide are both sold by the lineal foot. The term running foot is often substituted for lineal foot.

LINE LEVEL. See *level*.

LINTEL. A horizontal timber over a door or window opening which supports the walls directly above the opening. Lintels are usually made of two timbers 2-in. thick nailed together but can be made of one 4-in. timber. The width of the timbers ranges from 4 to 10 in., depending on the span.

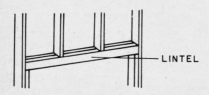

LIPPED DOOR. A cabinet door rabbeted on all four sides so that it fits part way into the door opening on the back side but overlaps the edges of the opening on the front side.

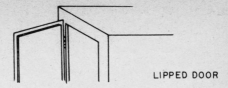

LIPPED DOOR

LIVE LOAD. See *load.*

LOAD. The weight that a timber or part of a structure, such as the floor or roof, carries.

Design load is the total load which a structure is de-signed to carry. *Dead,* or *static, load* is the weight of the permanent construction in a building and also the weight of objects, such as pianos, that are in a more or less permanent position. *Live load* is the weight of all moving and variable loads, such as a person walking, snow, wind, etc.

Although loads are of particular concern in buildings, they must also be considered when you construct furniture, cabinets and other things.

LOBLOLLY PINE. See *pine, southern yellow.*

LOCK. A device with the sole purpose of making doors secure (or reasonably so) against entrance by intruders. Compare *lockset.*

Locks for building doors can be recessed in the doors or mounted on the inner surface. The latter are generally called night locks. Some are operated only by a key, some only by a bolt on the inside of the door, and some by both key and bolt.

Locks for cabinets and furniture pieces are much smaller than door locks. All are key-controlled. Most are recessed in the wood for sake of appearance, but a few are surface-mounted.

LOCKSET. Locks for building doors which also operate as latches. The most reliable type and the most difficult for a burglar to open is the *mortise lockset.* In this, the latching and locking mechanism is enclosed in a cast-iron box which is mortised into the edge of a door. A rectangular deadbolt, which can be operated only by a key or a thumb-screw on the inside, locks the door.

Tubular and cylindrical locksets are more commonly used today because they are less expensive; but they are much less reliable and easy for a burglar to open. They should be used only on bathroom and other inside doors which are locked occasionally. Both are quickly installed by drilling a large hole through the faces of the door for the knobs and a small hole through the edge for the beveled tongue. The tongue is used for both latching and locking. In an ordinary snaplock, the tongue can be opened with a strip of celluloid. In a deadlatch the tongue is held rigid by a pin on the flat side. See *latch.*

LOCK-SET BIT. See *bit.*

LOCK WASHER. See *washer.*

LONGLEAF PINE. See *pine, southern yellow.*

LOUVER. One of a series of slanted boards used in shutters, doors, fences and louvered openings. In most uses, louvers are horizontal and designed to exclude precipitation and/or vision while admitting air and a certain amount of light. In louvered fences, however, the large louver boards are vertical—designed only to limit vision into the garden.

A louver is also a ventilation opening in an attic, soffit, exterior wall or basement.

LUMBER. Wood cut to a size and shape for ready use by carpenters, woodworkers, etc. Plywood is a form of lumber but differs so greatly from the solid boards and timbers originally sold as lumber that it is described separately.

Lumber is classified and described in various ways:

Softwood. Lumber cut from trees with needle-like leaves. See *softwood.*

Hardwood. Lumber cut from broad-leaved trees. See *hardwood.*

Flat-grain, plain-sawed and *slash-cut.* Lumber sawed from the log so that the growth rings form an angle of less than 45° with the wide faces of the lumber. See *grain.*

Edge-grain, quarter-sawed and *rift-cut.* Lumber sawed so that the growth rings form an angle of more than 45° with the wide faces of the lumber. See *grain.*

Rough lumber. Lumber that is not planed after sawing to shape and size.

Surfaced lumber. Also known as dressed lumber, this is lumber that has been run through a planer. The extent to which a piece has been surfaced is printed on it in a standardized code. For example, S2E means "surfaced 2 edges"; S2S, "surfaced 2 sides"; S2S1E, "surfaced 2 sides and 1 edge". As a rule, home craftsmen choose S4S stock which has been surfaced on all sides and edges.

One result of surfacing is that the actual size of lumber is somewhat less than the nominal size. How much less depends on how the lumber is graded for quality and on whether it is "dry" (seasoned to a point where it has a moisture content of 19% or less) or "green". In general, top-quality lumber is very slightly smaller than average lumber. For example, dry boards of nominal 1-in. thickness are actually 3/4 in. thick whereas green boards are 25/32 in. Board widths have a similar relationship (dimensions in inches):

Nominal	4	6	8	10	11	14
Dry	3-9/16	5-1/2	7-1/2	9-1/2	11-1/2	13-1/2
Green	3-5/8	5-5/8	7-5/8	9-3/4	11-3/4	13-3/4

The minimum length of most lumber is 6 ft. It ranges upward from this usually in multiples of 2 ft. but sometimes in increments of 1 ft.

Yard lumber. The major part of the softwood lumber sold in lumber yards. It is used primarily for light construction.

Dimension lumber. Yard lumber of any width and between 2 and 5 in. thick.

Finish lumber. Yard lumber of good appearance and finish.

Structural lumber. Softwood lumber for heavy construction. The smallest dimension of any piece is 5 in.

Factory or shop lumber. Lumber intended for further processing into such things as doors, furniture, etc.

Milled lumber. This is the name given some factory or shop lumber after further processing. See *millwork.*

In addition to these categories, lumber is sorted into grades. That in the top grades is called Select; in the lower grades, Common. The eight grades for softwood lumber are as follows:

B & Better or 1 & 2 Clear. Almost free of all blemishes and defects. It is used for the finest cabinet work.

C Select. Just a shade less perfect. Used for high-quality interior trim and cabinet work.

D Select. May have a few small knots, checks, etc.

1 Common. With some fairly large, sound, tight knots. This grade, however, is not commonly available except by special order.

2 Common. Very close to No. 1. It is used for knotty paneling and also for exterior trim.

3 Common. With larger knots and more of them, but used for shelving, paneling and siding.

4 Common. This is the most widely used grade in light construction, but the lumber is rarely exposed to view. It goes into subfloors, sheathing, etc.

5 Common. May have large knots, large holes, splits and other major defects. Not used very much by craftsmen.

Hardwood lumber is graded in similar fashion. The top grades are A Finish and B Finish, followed by No. 1, No. 2 and No. 3 Construction Boards.

Most lumber is priced by the board foot. But lumber less than 1/2 in. thick is sold by the square foot, while moldings and interior trim (among other items) are sold by the lineal foot.

M

MACHINE BOLT. See *bolt.*

MADRONE. A tough, heavy, pale pink wood with occasional deep red spots. It comes from the Pacific Coast and is sometimes used as a veneer in furniture and paneling.

MAGNETIC CATCH. See *catch.*

MAGNOLIA. This hard, heavy wood from the southern magnolia is very much like yellow poplar and used in the same ways.

MAHOGANY. Outstanding furniture and cabinet wood which is also used in paneling and boat building. True mahogany lumber comes from a Central American tree. The wood is deep red-brown, close-grained, highly figured, and has prominent growth rings and white mineral deposits in the pores after sanding. It is moderately hard and heavy, but easily worked.

MAIDOU. From Indochina, a high-priced furniture wood which is a pale yellowish color with ribbon stripes of red. It often has beautiful burls and crotches.

MAKORI. A well figured, lustrous, pale red African hardwood with dark red lines. It is dense, heavy, strong and easily worked. The main use is in furniture. It is also called African cherry.

MALLET. A hammering tool with a wide-faced, barrel-like head made of hard rubber or wood. Designed to prevent damage to the object being struck, mallets are

used to drive home pieces of wood in a structure and to hammer wood-handled chisels and gouges.

MAPLE. The wood of two types of maple is used for lumber—soft maple and hard maple. Soft maple goes into furniture to some extent but is weak and of little importance. Hard maple, however, is highly valued for furniture, cabinets, flooring and paneling. This is heavy, hard, strong and tough; light reddish-brown in color. The grain is generally straight but sometimes highly figured. Varieties known as bird's-eye, curly and wavy maple are prized for cabinet work.

MARKING GAUGE. See *gauge.*

MARKING KNIFE. See *utility knife.*

MARQUETRY. An inlay of woods of different colors.

MATCHED. An adjective applied to tongue-and-groove boards and boards with interlocking rabbets. The adjective is also applied to furniture or plywood veneers with matching grain or figure.

MAUL. A large, heavy hammer or mallet for driving stakes, spikes, etc.

MEDULLARY RAYS. The bands of cells extending from the center of a tree across the grain to the bark. They are inconspicuous in most woods, but prominent in others such as oak and beech. When these woods are quarter-sawed, the rays appear to be composed of many small flakes.

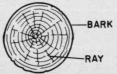

MENDING PLATE. In its broadest sense, a mending plate is any flat steel or brass plate that is screwed across a wood joint to strengthen it. But strictly speaking, a mending plate is a straight strip with four holes and ranging from 2 to 10 in. long.

Other plates are shaped like a T or an L. The former is properly known as a flat T plate; the latter, as a flat corner or an angle iron.

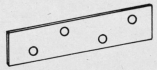

MILLED LUMBER. See *lumber*.

MILLWORK. Millwork includes lumber which has been milled to special shapes and also various assembled items such as doors and windows. Millwork may be produced to order to special designs but most of that sold today is of stock design. However, the stock designs, like women's fashions, are forever changing; consequently, if you want to match an old piece of stock millwork, the new material usually must be turned out especially for you.

MITER. To cut at any angle other than 90°. As a noun, miter means an obliquely cut surface.

MITER BOX. A device to simplify mitering of wood. In its simplest form it is a U-shaped trough of wood with 45° slots cut in the opposite sides to serve as saw guides. More elaborate miter boxes are actually L-shaped. The saw is held in metal guides which can be set, depending on the model, at any angle from 30° to 90°.

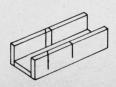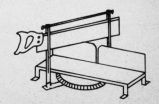

MITER JOINT. See *joint*.

MOLDING. A strip of wood, frequently of decorative design, that is used in a building strictly for decoration, to cover joints, or to serve some other practical purpose.

Base-cap moldings are applied to the tops of base-boards. *Shoe moldings,* sometimes called base shoes, are quarter-round strips covering the joints between base-boards and the floor.

Chair rail is a molding applied horizontally to walls to keep the backs of chairs from marring the walls.

Cornice molding is attached to the cornice or frieze on the outside of a house. It is also used at the top of interior walls.

Cove molding, a simple concave strip, is used under the front edges of stair treads, in corners of walls and wherever it is necessary to cover a joint in an inside corner.

Crown molding is attached under the eave of a roof. A *bed molding* is similar but used along the top of the frieze.

Half-round is a simple molding used to cover joints between various types of wall and ceiling panels. An *astragal* is a decorative molding used for the same purpose.

Nose molding is used to round off the front edges of stair treads.

Panel molding divides wall spaces into panels as if you nailed a large picture frame without any glass, picture or backing to the wall.

Picture molding at the top of a wall is used for hanging pictures.

Quarter-round is a molding used to cover inside corner joints.

Rake molding is attached under the rake of a roof.

Screen molding covers the edges of insect screening.

Two types of joint are used where moldings meet at corners. Coped joints are best for inside corners; miter joints for outside corners. See *joint*.

MOLLY SCREW. Also called a molly bolt or a hollow-wall screw anchor, a device for attaching things such as drapery brackets and towel rods to hollow walls and doors which will not hold nails or screws. It consists of a cylinder that is, as a rule, inserted into a drilled hole, and a bolt inserted first into the object to be attached and then into the cylinder. As the bolt is tightened, the walls of the cylinder mushroom out against the inside back surface of the wall. The screws come in several thicknesses and lengths for use in walls up to 1-3/4 in. thick.

MORTISE. A hole cut in a piece of wood to receive another piece of wood, a lock or anything else. As a verb, mortise means to cut such a hole.

Among people working with wood, the most familiar mortise is one cut to receive a tenon. See *joint.*

MORTISE AND TENON JOINT. See *joint.*

MORTISE BOLT. See *bolt, locking.*

MORTISING JIG. A device used with a router for mortising door jambs and edges for paumelle and olive knuckle hinges.

MOUNTS. The decorative and functional details, such as knobs and escutcheons, applied to a furniture piece or cabinet.

MYRTLE. A hard, strong wood with interesting burls which are sliced into handsome furniture veneers. These are greenish-yellow in color and often have purple blotches.

N

NAIL. In carpentry work the nail is the standard fastener, but it is less used in woodworking because it does not make such a strong, permanent joint as a screw, dowel or glue.

Most, but not all, nails are graded in size by the penny system. "Penny" is abbreviated by the letter "d." Stand-and-length nails are identified as follows (length given in inches):

Size	L	Size	L	Size	L	Size	L
2d	1	6d	2	10d	3	30d	4-1/2
3d	1-1/4	7d	2-1/4	12d	3-1/4	40d	5
4d	1-1/2	8d	2-1/2	16d	3-1/2	50d	5-1/2
5d	1-3/4	9d	2-3/4	20d	4	60d	6

The diameter of nail shanks increases with the total length of the nails. A 6-in. common nail, for example, has a diameter of approximately 9/32 in. A 1-1/2-in. nail, on the other hand, has a diameter of about 3/32 in.

Common nails have big, round, flat heads and are used in building work where, as a rule, the heads need not be concealed for appearances' sake (in framing and sheathing, for example). They come in all the sizes listed above except 5, 7 and 9 penny.

Wire nails are also shaped like common nails but have very thin, short shanks. They are used to nail together thin materials, such as lattice strips, when it is unnecessary to conceal the heads. They are sold by the inch, not by the penny. Lengths range from 5/8 to 1-1/4 in. Most lengths are made in several gauges.

Box nails are thin-gauge common nails used in building boxes and for light, rough construction. They are available with either a smooth or barbed shank, and are made in 3 to 8 penny sizes; also in 10, 16 and 20 penny sizes.

Finishing nails are thin nails with small, almost globular heads which are easily countersunk with a nailset. They are used for finishing work in construction and also in cabinet work. Available penny sizes are 3, 4, 6, 8 and 10.

Casing nails are similar to finishing nails but slightly thicker. They have cone-shaped heads. Penny sizes are 4, 6, 8, 10 and 16.

Many special-purpose nails are used in construction. The following are the more important:

Cut nails are tapering, rectangular nails used to put down strip flooring.

Screw nails have a steep, spiral thread to increase holding power. They are used for laying floors as well as for other purposes when great rigidity is called for. They have small heads.

Ring-grooved, or *ringed-shank, nails* have large, flat heads and concentric grooves on the shanks to increase holding power. They are most often used to install gypsum board panels.

Shingle nails are short common nails with very sharp points. They are always galvanized.

Roofing nails are short, galvanized common nails with extra large heads and sharp points.

Double-headed nails are common nails with an extra head about 1/4 in. above the regular head. They are designed for temporary work because they are easy to pull. *Scaffolding nails* are similar, but the upper head resembles that of a finishing nail.

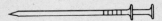

Nails are made of bright steel, galvanized steel, stainless steel, aluminum, bronze and monel. They are sometimes given a special finish to alter their appearance, affect their corrosion resistance or increase their holding power.

NAIL CLAW. A straight piece of stout, round or hexagonal steel with one end curved. The curved end is flattened and has a slot for pulling nails.

This tool is similar to a ripping bar but is smaller and does not have a chisel end as well as a claw.

NAIL-HOLDING POWER. The ability of wood to keep nails driven into it from pulling loose when the wood is under stress is important to everyone working with wood; consequently, all woods are measured for their nail-holding power. In general, the harder the wood, the greater its power. Oak, for instance, has a much higher rating in this respect than spruce.

NAIL PULLER. A heavy mechanical device designed to simplify the pulling of nails which have been driven flush with a wood surface or below it. It has a pincer-like jaws on the end of a handle. When the handle is pushed down, the jaws nip in under the nail head and grasp it firmly. The puller is then used as a lever to withdraw the nail.

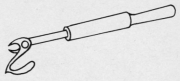

NAILSET. The conventional nailset is a small, rigid steel punch with a concave (cupped) tip which is used to countersink nails. Tip sizes range from 1/32 to 5/32 in.

A self-centering nailset, designed to speed nailsetting and prevent accidental marring of the wood, has a hollow tip which is slipped down over the nail head. A plunger in the back of the tool is then struck with a hammer to drive the nail below the surface of the wood. The plunger retracts between blows.

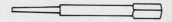

NEST OF SAWS. A collection of small saw blades to be used interchangeably in the same handle.

NEWEL POST. The large post at the bottom or top of a stair railing. It is the principal support for the handrail and is sometimes the only support.

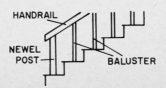

HANDRAIL

NEWEL
POST

BALUSTER

NOMINAL SIZE. The stated size of a piece of lumber. In many cases, the actual size is smaller. See *lumber*.

NONBEARING PARTITION. An interior wall which does not support the joists above it. It serves only as a space divider. Compare *bearing partition*.

NON-MORTISE HINGE. See *hinge*.

NOSE MOLDING. See *molding*.

NOSING. A wood edge that has been rounded, like the front edge of a stair tread.

O

OAK. Oak lumber is identified either as white oak or red oak. Both are heavy, hard, strong, tough woods. White oak, however, is more refined in appearance and more resistant to decay. It has somewhat closed pores; is grayish- to reddish-brown. It is prized for furniture, cabinet work, paneling, trim and is used to some extent in flooring. Red oak is coarse-grained and redder. It is used mainly in flooring although it is by no means limited to this.

OFFSET. A surface not in the same plane as the larger surrounding surface. A raised or sunken panel in a wall is an offset, for example.

OFFSET SCREWDRIVER. See *screwdriver*.

OGEE. A molding with a more or less S-shaped curve.

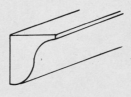

OIL-BASE PUTTY. See *putty*.

OILSTONE. A whetstone used for finish sharpening of cutting tools. It is treated with oil to prevent the tiny steel particles ground off tools from clogging the pores of the stone. Oilstones are usually artificial but may be made of natural stone—most commonly Arkansas stone or Washita stone.

Slipstones are oil stones shaped to fit the inside curves of gouges. If a slipstone is tapered, it can be used to sharpen gouges of several sizes.

OLIVE. A dense, hard, heavy, close-grained wood used for carving and inlays. It has a yellowish- or greenish-brown background streaked with dark brown lines.

OLIVE KNUCKLE HINGE. See *hinge*.

ON CENTERS. A term used to describe the spacing of studs, joists and rafters. The space is measured not from the side of one timber to the side of the adjoining timber but from the center of the front edge of one timber to the center of the front edge of the next timber. The timbers are then said to be "16 in. (or whatever the actual distance) on centers". On plans, this is written: 16″ O.C.

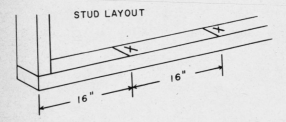

STUD LAYOUT

OPENWORK. Any furniture part, cabinet part, ornamental screen, etc. which has openings that you can see through. Most openwork is decorative.

ORIENTALWOOD. A brown or pinkish-gray Australian furniture wood resembling black walnut. It is very difficult to work with ordinary tools but is frequently sliced into veneers.

OUT OF TRUE. Not in the proper position. For example, a door hanging on a slant and a sloping ceiling are out of true.

OUTSIDE CORNER. A corner forming an angle of more than 180°, such as the corner of a table. It is also called an external corner, and is the opposite of an internal, or inside, corner.

P

PADAUK. An extremely strong, hard, heavy wood with big, open pores. It has a straw-colored or pink background accented by red and reddish-brown streaks. It is used in furniture.

PALDAO. A Philippine hardwood of unusually variable appearance which is used in furniture and gunstocks. The background color is pink-gray or yellow-gray. This is overlaid with irregular mottling or streaks of several dark colors.

PANELING. An interior wall or ceiling covering made of wood, plywood, or composition materials. There is tremendous variation in the design not only of paneling materials but also of the paneled surfaces. The simplest wood paneling consists of flat boards usually with chamfered edges nailed side by side vertically to walls or sloping ceilings. In the simplest plywood paneling, the sheets are applied vertically and the joints are either left open or covered with moldings.

PANEL MOLDING. See *molding*.

PARE. To remove wood with chisels or other tools in thin shavings.

PARING GOUGE. See *gouge*.

PARLIAMENT HINGE. See *hinge*.

PARQUET. A wood floor constructed of small blocks laid in a decorative pattern. See *flooring*.

PARTICLEBOARD. Also called chipboard and flakeboard, this is a panel (usually 4 by 8 ft. and of several thicknesses) made of wood chips bonded together under pressure. It is smooth, quite strong, and has an attractive textured look; but its principal virtue is its exceptional resistance to warping, shrinking and expanding. It is used for cabinet doors, table and desk tops; and as a base for plastic laminates and resilient flooring.

PARTING TOOL. A narrow-bladed wood-turning tool used for cutting grooves and recesses. See *gouge.*

PATINA. The mellow color which wood acquires with age.

PAUMELLE HINGE. See *hinge.*

PEAR. Pearwood is a very light rosy-pink with dark and light shadings. It is tough, extremely hard and fine-grained. It is used in furniture and turnings.

PECAN. A heavy, hard, strong type of hickory of medium-brown color and with an attractive, variable grain. It is popular for cabinets and furniture.

PECK. A channeled or pitted area in wood. It is most often seen in cedar.

PEG. To put together with wood pegs instead of metal fasteners. Pegs are also called pins.

PEN KNIFE. See *pocket knife.*

PENNY. A nail size. It is abbreviated by the letter "d." A six-penny, or 6d, nail is 2 in. long, for instance. Originally the word indicated the price of 100 nails.

PEROBA. Two Brazilian furniture woods—one a pale rose color with yellow shadings as in a peach; the other, pale yellow with a slight brownish cast and distinctive mottling.

PHILIPPINE MAHOGANY. A soft, light hardwood, rather closely grained. It ranges from reddish- to grayish-brown in color and has light and dark striping. It is widely used in hardwood paneling, also—to some extent—in furniture. This is not a true mahogany. The trees which are the principal sources of the wood are the lauan and tanguile.

PIANO HINGE. See *hinge*.

PICTURE MOLDING. See *molding*.

PIER. A square or round masonry column used to support other structural members. It is built up from a wide masonry footing which is normally placed below the frost line.

PILOT HOLE. The hole drilled in wood to receive the threaded section of a screw. A larger hole may be made for the shank and a still larger hole for the head. Drills called countersinks are designed to make the three holes in one operation.

A pilot hole is also a hole drilled part way through a board to receive a nail which might split the board if it were driven in in the usual manner.

PIN. A wooden peg or dowel.

PINCERS. A pliers-like tool with jaws like a human's. It is useful for pulling nails and tacks or cutting off the heads.

PINE, SOUTHERN YELLOW. The principal species yielding southern yellow pine lumber—sometimes known simply as yellow pine—are the longleaf pine, shortleaf pine, loblolly pine and slash pine. The wood is heavy, hard, yellowish, resinous and straight-grained. It is difficult to work and does not take paint well, but has excellent strength and is extensively used in construction and to make softwood plywood. The heartwood—especially of longleaf pine—has moderately good resistance to decay.

PINE, WHITE. The four species which are the principal sources of white pine lumber are the eastern white pine, western white pine, sugar pine and ponderosa pine. The differences between the four woods are not pronounced, although the eastern white pine is generally considered the best—especially for fine carpentry and cabinet work —while the western white pine is the strongest.

In general, white pine is a soft, light-weight, light-colored wood with a close, straight grain. It is very easy to work and takes paint well; is the ideal wood for interior and exterior trim, windows, doors and pattern-making.

PITCH. The slope of a roof. It is measured and stated in the number of inches it rises in each horizontal foot. For instance, a roof that rises 3 in. per foot is said to have a 3-in. pitch or a 3-in-12 rise. On a plan, this may be written 3:12.

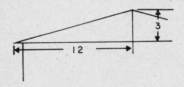

PITCH STREAK. An accumulation of pitch (resin) in a well defined streak.

PITH. Soft, spongy tissue at the very center of tree trunks and limbs. Lumber containing a great deal of pith should not be used for structural purposes.

PIVOT HINGE. See *hinge.*

PLAIN-SAWED. Hardwood lumber which has been sawed so that the growth rings form an angle of less than 45° with the wide faces. See *grain.*

PLANE. Tool for taking down wood, smoothing rough surfaces, shaping, rabbeting, routing and grooving. Although some of the more specialized planes do not closely resemble those in common use, all are assembled and used in much the same way. The angle of the cutting blade, called the plane iron, is controlled by the design of the plane. (For example, in large planes the iron is set at an angle of 45° from horizontal, whereas the angle in many block planes is only 12° or 20°). The depth of the cut, however, is readily adjusted up and down with the adjusting nut.

The following types of plane are in use:

The *jack plane*, normally operated with two hands, is the best all-round plane because it is small enough for easy handling when you are trimming wood to size and smoothing it, yet it is long enough to ride over any unevenness in a board and make a straight cut. (Short planes, by contrast, follow the contours of the wood.) Jack planes are 14 to 15 in. long and have a 2-in. plane iron.

The *junior jack plane* is similar to the jack but only 11-1/2 in. long. It has a 1-3/4-in. plane iron.

The *smooth plane* is an 8- or 9-in. jack plane used for exact work on fairly short pieces of wood.

The *fore plane* and *jointer plane* are also like the jack plane. The former is 18 in. long; the latter, 22 in. Both have 2-3/8-in.-wide plane irons.

The *block plane* is used in one hand to smooth end-grain and for other small jobs. It is 6 or 7 in. long; has a plane iron 1-5/8 in. wide.

Trimming planes are imprecise tools but useful for very small work. They are 3 in. long; have a cutter 1 in. wide.

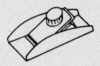

The *rabbet plane* has a 1-in. cutting blade for rabbeting boards. The plane is designed with straight, flat sides at right angles to the bottom so it can be placed on either side to cut the edge of a board. The plane is 5-1/2 in. long.

The *bullnose rabbet plane* is used for the same work but the cutting edge is only a fraction of an inch back from the toe so that you can cut up close to an obstruction. The plane is 4 in. long and has a 1-in. cutter.

In a *duplex rabbet plane* there are two seats for the 1-1/2-in. cutter. One seat is for regular rabbeting; the other, for bullnose work. Included are an adjustable fence and a depth gauge. The plane is 8-1/2 in. long.

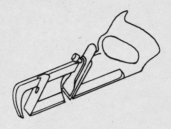

The *side rabbet plane* incorporates two 1/2-in. blades pointed in opposite directions. One cuts on the forward stroke; the other on the return. The plane is used for trimming or smoothing grooves and dadoes.

The *router plane* is used to clean the wood out of dadoes and grooves after the sides have been sawed. The blades are L-shaped. The upright shank is attached to a cutting post and is adjustable up and down. The cutting edge is at the bottom tip of the L. The plane comes with three interchangeable blades. Two have chisel edges; one, a V edge.

The *small router plane* is a rectangular unit only 3 in. long with a single adjustable blade. It is used for inlaying and other small jobs.

The *plow plane* is for grooving wood which has not previously been cut. Blades of several widths are used. The plane has an adjustable fence.

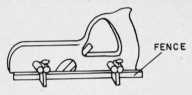

FENCE

The *circular plane* has a flexible metal bottom which can be adjusted exactly to a convex or concave curve. The cutter is 1-3/4 in. wide.

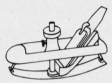

The *soft and hardboard plane* is made for beveling the edges of insulating boards and hardboard panels, and for cutting grooves. The cutters resemble razor blades and are replaced when they get dull.

PLANE, POWER. Portable smoothing tool for dressing rough lumber. A high-speed motor mounted on the side or top turns a revolving cutter blade roughly 2 in. wide. The plane can be adjusted to cut to a maximum depth of 3/32 in.

PLANER. A large machine for smoothing rough lumber. It is used by mills and lumber yards. Home craftsmen use jointers for the same purpose.

PLANK. A piece of lumber 2 to 4 in. thick and at least 6 in. wide.

PLANK FLOORING. See *flooring*.

PLASTIC ANCHOR. See *rawl plug*.

PLASTIC-RESIN GLUE. See *glue*.

PLASTIC WOOD. Wood-like dough used to fill holes in wood and plywood.

PLATE. A horizontal framing member nailed to the top of studs in order to support the joists or rafters above. Plates are usually made of 2 x 4s laid flat one atop the other.

In recent years, the Federal Housing Administration has extended the meaning of plate to cover all "horizontal wood members which provide bearing and anchorage for wall, floor, ceiling and roof framing.

"Sill plate: Plate on top of foundation wall which supports wood framing.

"Wall plate: Plate at top or bottom of wall or partition framing. Further defined as top plate, at top, and sole plate, at bottom.

"Rafter or joist plate: Plate at top of masonry or concrete wall supporting rafter or roof joist and ceiling framing."

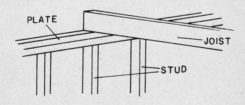

PLIERS. A gripping, turning and cutting tool available in many designs, but little used by carpenters and woodworkers except to tighten or loosen nuts and bend flashing. For these purposes, a pair of *slip-joint pliers* is all you need. The jaws can not only be opened in normal scissors fashion; but because of a slip joint, they can be adjusted to two or three positions so you can get a grip on large objects. The size and design of the jaws vary from model to model. Some models also can be used for cutting wire.

A related tool of occasional value is a *combination pliers*, sometimes called a plier-wrench. This can be used as a pliers and it can also be locked on to an object like a pipe wrench.

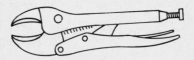

PLOW. To cut a lengthwise groove in a piece of wood.

PLOW PLANE. See *plane*.

PLUG CUTTER. A small tool used in a power drill to cut out hardwood plugs for subsequent insertion in a pegged floor or other pegged surface. The plugs cover the heads of screws recessed below the surface.

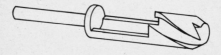

PLUMB LINE. A weighted piece of string used to mark a vertical line, to check whether a door frame, wall panel, etc. is vertical, or to find a point in the middle of a surface below a known point overhead. The weight made specifically for use on a plumb line is called a plumb bob; but any small weighted object can be substituted for this.

If a plumb line is used to mark a line in a wall, it is coated with chalk. When the plumb bob stops swinging, you hold it against the wall with one hand, pull the line out a few inches with the other hand, and let it snap against the wall.

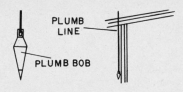

PLY. One of the wood layers in plywood or any other laminated piece.

PLYWOOD. A strong, rigid, durable, stable, flat sheet material made of three, five or seven plies of wood. It is extensively used for sheathing, subflooring, exterior walls, interior paneling, cabinets, built-ins, furniture, boat hulls, etc.

Softwood plywood was formerly called fir plywood because it was made only of Douglas fir; but it is now made from a number of woods. Since it is essentially a utility material and not very attractive, its greatest use is in the substructures of buildings and for other types of basic construction; but the building industry is making increasing use of panels which have a decorative texture and are designed to cover exterior or interior walls.

The standard size of softwood plywood panels is 4 by 8 ft. but some types are made in other sizes. Available thicknesses (but not in all types of panel) are 1/4, 5/16, 3/8, 1/2, 5/8, 3/4, 7/8, 1, 1-1/8, and 1-1/4 in.

The grading of softwood plywood is enormously complicated. The most important basic difference between types is in the adhesives binding the plies together. If the adhesive is not waterproof, the plywood is designated as an interior grade and must not be used outdoors or in a damp location indoors. Exterior plywood, on the other hand, is made with waterproof adhesive and can be used anywhere.

Both interior and exterior plywoods are subdivided into grades according to the quality of the face veneers. The following letters are used:

N — special-order veneer suitable for a natural finish. It is free of open defects; made of select wood which is either all heartwood or all sapwood.

A — Smooth and paintable, and may be given a natural finish in less demanding situations. Neatly made repairs in the veneer are permitted.

B — A solid, paintable veneer in which circular repair plugs and tight knots are permitted.

C — This is the minimum veneer used in exterior plywood. Limited splits and knot holes to 1-in. diameter (and under certain circumstances to 1-1/2 in.) are permitted.

C Plugged — Like the above, but the knot holes are filled with plugs to give a smooth surface.

D — Used only in interior plywood for the inner plies and backs.

When these letters appear in the identifying label stamped on each piece of plywood, the first indicates the grade given the veneer on the face of the panel; the second, the grade of the back panel. For example, B-D means that the face veneer is solid but that the back veneer has holes.

Hardwood plywood is also made of three, five or seven plies. Of these, the face veneer is a hardwood (although it is sometimes a softwood such as knotty pine); and in a few instances, the veneer on the back face may also be a hardwood. As a rule, these outer veneers are plain-sliced or quarter-sliced—meaning that they were sawed from the log, or flitch, in straight slices (like boards) and glued to the plywood base side by side. But rotary-cut veneers which are peeled from the circumference of a log, like a potato skin, are sometimes used— especially in birch plywood.

The material used for the inner plies depends on the construction of the panels. In common veneer-core plywood, the inner plies are roughly the same thickness as the outer plies and made either of softwood or hardwood. In lumber-core plywood, the center ply is a great deal thicker than the face plies and made usually of basswood or poplar boards glued edge to edge. In particleboard-core plywood, the center ply is also very thick but made of particleboard. These last two plywoods are used primarily in cabinetwork. There are also mineral-core plywoods used in fire-retardant construction.

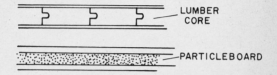

LUMBER CORE

PARTICLEBOARD

The main use for hardwood plywood is as an interior paneling, but it is also used extensively in cabinets, furniture, boats, etc.

Panels are 24, 30, 36, 42 and 48 in. wide; 4, 5, 6, 7 and 8 ft. long; and 1/8, 3/16, 1/4, 5/16, 3/8, 1/2, 5/8, 3/4, 13/16, 7/8 and 1 in. thick.

Panels are graded Good 1 Side (G1S) and Good 2 Sides (G2S). The "good" actually means that the veneer is of excellent quality.

POCKET. A crack between two growth rings. If it contains pitch—as it often does—it is called a pitch pocket.

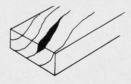

POCKET KNIFE. A knife with folding blades which is carried in the pocket. Small sizes are called pen knives; large sizes, jack knives. The extent to which a carpenter or woodworker uses a pocket knife seems to depend on how much he used one as a boy. To some men it is an indispensable tool; to others, simply a tool for sharpening a pencil if they do not happen to have a real sharpener handy.

POLYVINYL-RESIN GLUE. See *glue*.

PONDEROSA PINE. See *pine, white*.

POPLAR. The true poplars have weak, inferior wood. The only species used to any extent are the cottonwood and aspen, or silver poplar. The wood of the former is used in making boxes. The latter has a soft, light, close-grained wood with white sapwood and tan heartwood that is often streaked with brown. The choicest aspen wood is cut from the crotches and is used in furniture. Also see *yellow poplar*.

POST. A vertical timber used to support a load. Wood posts are at least 5 in. thick and 5 in. wide.

POWER-BORE BIT. See *bit*.

PRIMAVERA. A Central American cabinet and paneling wood closely resembling mahogany except in color. It is creamy white and is often known as white mahogany.

PRODUCTION PAPER. See *sandpaper*.

PROFILE. The contour of a molding, wall—anything at all.

PROTRACTOR. A small, thin, flat, half-round instrument for measuring and marking angles. The arc is graduated from 0° to 180°.

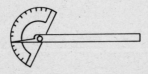

PRY BAR. A straight piece of heavy steel with one end shaped like a chisel and the other end tapering to a point. It is used for prying.

PULL. Any type of knob or handle for pulling open a drawer or cabinet door. It has no latching or catching mechanism.

PULL SCRAPER. See *scraper*.

PUMICE. A fine stone grit used as an abrasive to complete the finishing of handsome furniture and cabinets.

PUNCH. Small, steel tool used by people working with wood to make starting holes for screws and drill bits. A center punch is a piece of solid steel with a sharp point. A self-centering screwhole punch is used to make pilot holes for screws exactly in the center of the screw holes in hinges, strikeplates, etc. This is done by placing the rounded point of the punch in the screw hole and striking a loose pin in the back of the punch with a hammer.

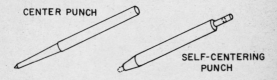

PURLIN. A timber nailed between two rafters at right angles to them. Purlins support planks and narrow insulating slabs which are laid up and down the roof to form the roof deck. When metal roofing is used, it is laid directly over the purlins.

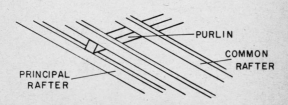

PURPLEHEART. See *amaranth*.

PUSH BOARD. A piece of wood used to push a board through a circular saw, jointer, etc. It is a safety device.

PUSH DRILL. See *drill*.

PUTTY. Three kinds of putty are used as fillers. *Oil-base putty* is the standard type made for generations. Even in its most pliable state, it is rather stiff; and it hardens to rock-like consistency.

Latex putty is more commonly called elastic putty because it remains reasonably soft for many years. Its primary use is in setting window panes.

Water, or *wood, putty* is sold as a plaster-like powder that is mixed with water. It sets within 30 min. and is completely dry and hard in 24 hr. It is used for filling holes; but is valuable principally because it can be molded into intricate shapes before it sets. Thus it is suitable for patching carved moldings, column capitals and other ornate articles.

PUTTY KNIFE. A tool for applying putty, spackle and similar materials in holes, cracks and dents. It has a flexible steel blade about 1 in. wide and with a squared end.

Q

QUARTER-ROUND. A simple molding shaped like a quarter of a circle. It is used primarily to cover joints between baseboards and floors and in inside corners. Sizes range from 1/2 by 1/2 in. to 1-1/16 by 1-1/16 in. Some quarter-rounds are greater in one dimension than the other and are not perfect quarter-rounds.

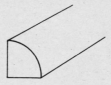

QUARTER-SAWED. Hardwood lumber which has been sawed so that the growth rings are at an angle of 45° or more to the wide faces. See *grain*.

QUIRK. A little groove separating a molding or bead from an adjoining surface. Also a groove separating two parts of a molding. An interruption.

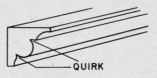

QUIRK

R

RABBET. A rectangular groove in the edge of a board, piece of plywood or other material. See *joint*.

RABBET JOINT. See *joint*.

RABBET PLANE. See *plane*.

RADIAL-ARM SAW. See *saw, shop*.

RADIAL BAR. A strip of wood with a nail driven through one end and a pencil attached to the other end. It is used for drawing large circles and curves. See *trammel points*.

RAFTER. One of the sloping timbers that support roofs with a 3 in 12 pitch or greater. (Joists are used in roofs with less pitch.) Depending on the weight of the roof and the space to be spanned, rafters are made of 2-in.-thick timbers 4, 6, 8 or 10 in. wide. They are normally spaced 16 in. on centers, but may be spaced 12 or 24 in. on centers.

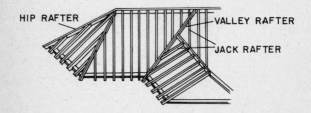

Common rafters run at right angles from the ridge to the rafter plates at the top of exterior walls.

A *hip rafter* is one of the corner rafters in a hip roof. It extends from the end of the ridge to the top of the exterior walls where they meet at a corner.

A *valley rafter* is one just beneath a valley formed by the meeting of two roof slopes.

Jack rafters are shortened common rafters. A hip jack extends at right angles from the rafter plate to a hip rafter. A valley jack extends at right angles from the ridge to a valley rafter. A cripple jack extends either from one valley rafter to another valley rafter or from a valley rafter to a hip rafter.

RAFTER PLATE. The horizontal timber on which the lower ends of rafters rest.

RAIL. The horizontal member of a fence. The top piece of a balustrade. The horizontal parts of a door; also the large horizontal top and bottom members of a window sash. The top horizontal piece between table legs (also called an apron).

RAISED PANEL. A sunken panel with a raised center in a door or wall. Compare *recessed panel*.

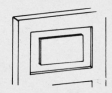

RAKE. The sloped end of a roof. Also the angle of the legs or back of a piece of furniture.

RAKE

RAKE MOLDING. See *molding*.

RANDOM WIDTH. Term applied to flooring boards and wall and ceiling paneling boards which are of several widths and are installed in no set sequence.

RASP. Tool very similar to a file but with individual coarse, triangular teeth arranged in rows. They are used for shaping wood prior to finishing.

Rasps are generally flat on one side; rounded on the other. Special shapes are available. Also, see *riffler*.

RATCHET BRACE. See *bit brace*.

RAWL PLUG. A small device made of wood fiber surrounding a cylinder of thin metal which is used mainly to attach things to plaster and gypsum board walls. It can also be used to hold screws in wood in cases where the original screwholes have become enlarged. The plug is inserted in a hole made in the wall or other surface; and as a screw of the proper size is driven into it, it expands and grips tight against the sides of the hole.

Plastic anchors and lead anchors are similar to rawl plugs but are not used for fastening to wood. Lead shields, as opposed to lead anchors, are used for fastening lag bolts.

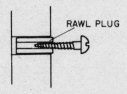

RAWL PLUG

RECESSED PANEL. A flat sunken panel in a door or wall. Compare *raised panel*.

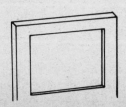

RECIPROCATING-ORBITAL SANDER. See *sander.*

RECIPROCATING SAW. See *saw, portable power.*

RED OAK. See *oak.*

REDWOOD. A moderately soft, light, reddish wood with straight grain. It is highly resistant to decay and termites; is easy to work, and holds paint well. It is popular in the construction industry, especially on the Pacific Coast. It is also used to make outdoor furniture.

REEDING. Molding made to resemble reeds.

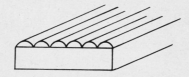

RELIEF CUT. One of several preliminary cuts made in a piece of wood with a bandsaw or saber saw so the saw can cut a sharp curve.

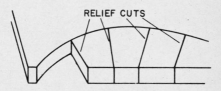

RELIEF CUTS

RESORCINOL GLUE. See *glue.*

RIBBON STRIP. A horizontal timber nailed to the face of studs to support floor joists. In an existing building, it may also be nailed to the face of a wall to support the joists for an addition. Ribbon strip and ledger are interchangeable words.

RIDGE. The horizontal timber at the peak of a gable, gambrel, hip or Mansard roof. It ties the rafters together at their upper ends and helps to align them. Illustrated at *rafter*.

RIFFLER. A metal rod with a small, oddly shaped rasp at each end. It is used in wood carving for working corners and recesses. Many styles are made.

RIFT-CUT. See *grain*.

RINGED-SHANK NAIL. See *nail*.

RING-GROOVED NAIL. See *nail*.

RIP. To saw with the grain.

RIPPING BAR. A heavy, stout, very strong tool used for prying, pulling large immovable nails and tearing things apart. It is often called a wrecking bar.

The conventional bar has a gooseneck with a nail slot at one end. The other end is slightly curved and beveled to a chisel edge.

Another type of bar is called a ripping chisel because it has a wider chisel end. The chisel end also has nail slot as well as a wedge-shaped hole that is used for nail pulling. One version of this tool has a gooseneck at the opposite end; another version is straight from end to end so you can strike it with a hammer.

Still another kind of ripping bar is a short, heavy steel strap with both ends sharpened to a chisel edge, two nail slots and one nail hole.

RIP SAW. See *saw*.

RISER. The vertical board under the front of a stair tread.

ROOFING NAIL. See *nail.*

ROSEWOOD. Rosewood is the name applied to several types of trees and their woods. The most important varieties are Brazilian and Madagascar rosewood. These are a deep ruddy to purplish brown with almost-yellow and black streaks. They are easy to carve but are otherwise difficult to work. Good supplies of Brazilian rosewood are available; but Madagascar rosewood is scarce.

ROTARY JOINTER-SURFACER. An electrically driven shop tool with a vertically mounted cutting wheel. It is used for planing wood up to 6 in. wide or thick, and also for jointing, beveling, chamfering, trimming and tapering. The table can be adjusted from 90° to 45°.

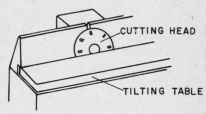

CUTTING HEAD

TILTING TABLE

ROTTENSTONE. An abrasive powder used to give furniture and cabinet work a beautiful finish.

ROUND. A long, circular piece of wood such as a dowel or broom handle. As a verb, round (or more often, round off) means to cut off a sharp edge or square corner to produce a rounded profile.

ROUTER. Extremely versatile, motor-driven tool used to make joints, shape edges, cut grooves, mortise, rout out areas in wood or plywood, inlay and make templets and fancy shapes.

Routers are round, upright tools with handles on two sides. They move on a flat, circular steel base with a large hole through which the bits project. The motors operate at from about 18,000 to 27,000 rpm, depending on the model.

The interchangeable bits are of many designs and shapes but are made either for grooving or cutting edges. The depth of the cut they make can be regulated.

Many other accessories are also used with routers. Of these, the most basic are a guide attachment which follows the edge of a board or panel, and a templet guide for following the outlines of a templet.

In addition to being operated in normal base-down position, routers can be installed under a workbench top and used upside down as table shapers. In some cases, they can also be used to run a power plane attachment.

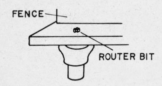

FENCE

ROUTER BIT

ROUTER PLANE. See *plane*.

RULE. One-piece, rigid wood *bench rules*. are made in 6-, 12- and 24-in. lengths. They are the basic measuring instrument for woodworkers while the basic instruments for carpenters are either wood *folding rules* or steel *tape rules*. The former are made in 6-in. sections hinged together. They open out to a maximum length of 6 or 8 ft. The best rules have a slide-out, tongue-like extension rule for making fast inside measurements of openings, such as doors or closets.

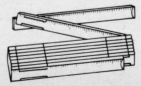

Tape rules are flexible steel tapes which slide in and out of compact cases. In some models, the tape retracts automatically when a button is pressed. The rules are available in lengths of 6, 8, 10, 12, 16, 20 and 25 ft. They have gained in popularity at the expense of folding rules because of their length, durability, ease of opening and closing, and small size when closed. On the other hand, because they lack the stiffness of folding rules, they are not always as easy to handle and they are difficult to use to make horizontal measurements if there is nothing to lay them on.

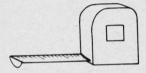

Another type of rule is a wood *extension-stick*—a two-section sliding rule that extends from 5 to as much as 10 ft. Its main use is for measuring boards and timbers, such as studs, which are cut repeatedly to a specific size over a period of time.

RUSTIC SIDING. A board with bevel edges on the front side. When applied either horizontally or vertically to exterior walls, there are rather wide, deep V joints between adjoining boards. The edges of the boards also interlock to keep out water.

S

SABER SAW. See *saw, portable power*.

SAMARA. See *gaboon*.

SANDER. Electric hand tool designed to give wood and plywood a smooth finish. Three types are in use.

The *reciprocating-orbital sander* has a flat sanding base which works forward and backward in very short, rapid strokes. For fast sanding, the tool has an orbital action—meaning that it goes back and forth in all directions. For finish sanding, it has a straight front-and-back reciprocating action. (Separate reciprocating and orbital sanders are on the market, but the dual-action machine is understandably more popular.)

Belt sanders are equipped with endless abrasive belts that operate at high speed and are capable—if the operator isn't careful—of cutting deep grooves in wood. They are best used on large surfaces which need more smoothing and leveling than can be done with a dual-action sander. The top models have two speeds.

Disk sanders have revolving sanding disks up to 7 in. across; but the tools known by this name are made primarily for sanding, grinding and polishing metals.

All *electric drills*, however, can be converted to sanders by inserting a circular semi-flexible rubber disk or a ball-jointed metal disk in the chuck to serve as a base for the sandpaper. The former is better for sanding curved surfaces; the latter, for flat surfaces. But in both cases, results are far from perfect because this kind of sander has an aggressive action which leaves circular scratches in all surfaces. For another sanding device used in electric drills, see *Sand-O-Flex*.

SANDER-GRINDER. See *sanding machine*.

SANDING BLOCK. Any device used to hold sandpaper to facilitate even sanding of a surface. You would use a flat wood block, for instance, to sand a flat surface; a piece of broom handle to sand a curved, square-edged surface. Rubber-faced sanding blocks with clamps to hold the paper are sold in hardware stores for use on flat surfaces.

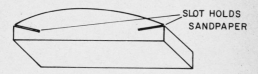

SLOT HOLDS
SANDPAPER

SANDING MACHINE. An electrically driven shop tool not often found in home workshops, but of use if you do a great deal of woodworking. The smallest machines are mentioned here:

The *small belt sander* has an endless sanding belt about 6 in. wide perpendicular to the work table.

The *sander-grinder* is similar but has a belt only about 1 in. wide and is used mainly for small and intricate jobs.

The *disk sander* has a large, vertical sanding disk.

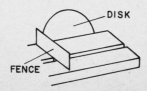

DISK

FENCE

The *spindle sander* has a small-diameter, vertical sanding drum centered in the work table. It is useful for sanding cut-outs.

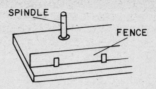

The *combination sander* has both a 9-in. disk and 6-in. belt.

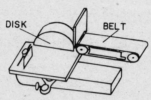

SAND-O-FLEX. A patented device which can be attached to an electric drill for sanding contoured surfaces such as moldings and turnings. It resembles a small water wheel with flexible, comb-tooth-like abrasive strips projecting from the "buckets". The wheel is usually operated at drill speeds of 2000 rpm or less. The abrasive strips, available in several grits, are replaceable when they wear out.

SANDPAPER. Sandpapers used for hand-smoothing and finishing wood and plywood include flint paper, production paper, garnet paper and silicon-carbide paper.

Flint paper uses silica as a grit and is light brown in color. It wears badly, but because it is cheap, it is widely used for sanding painted and varnished surfaces that clog all sandpapers.

Production paper has an aluminum-oxide grit. It lasts many times longer than flint paper and also cuts much faster. It is the standard sandpaper for finishing wood. It is also the paper used most often in electric sanders.

Silicon-carbide paper is the toughest of all. A waterproof paper, it can be used for wet as well as dry sanding. It is particularly good for fine work.

Garnet paper is similar to silicon-carbide paper but not quite so tough.

Sandpaper is graded by the coarseness of the grit. Nos. 16 through 40 are called "coarse"; Nos. 50 through 100, "medium"; Nos. 120 through 240, "fine"; Nos. 280 through 320, "very fine"; and Nos. 360 through 600, "polishing".

The standard size sheet measures 9 by 11 in.; but collections of sandpapers are put up in quarter-size pieces.

SAPELE. A dark red-brown African hardwood rather widely used as a furniture wood but of little value as lumber because of its tendency to warp. If a log is cut longitudinally through the center, the wood has a striped appearance.

SAPWOOD. The young wood just inside the bark of a tree trunk or limb. It forms a ring around the older heartwood, and is usually lighter in color. The actual width of the ring depends on the type of tree and its age.

Sapwood is as strong as heartwood but is often less resistant to decay and therefore less durable.

SATINWOOD. A durable, hard, very close-grained, pale yellow wood from Ceylon. Used in furniture veneers, it has a lustrous sheen and beautiful striped and mottled figure. The dust of the wood is poisonous.

SAW, HAND. If a saw is to be useful for cutting wood and plywood over a period of many years, it must be made of flexible, tempered steel. The teeth are alternately bent to left and right to make a kerf slightly wider than the blade thickness. This prevents binding. Further to prevent binding, the blade is made slightly thicker at the toothed edge than at the back.

Several kinds of saw are used by carpenters and woodworkers.

The *crosscut saw* for cutting across the grain of wood and for all cutting of plywood has small teeth with knife-like points. Saws with eight points per inch are used for coarse work; those with ten points, for fine work. Twelve-point saws are called panel saws and used for very fine work. Blades range from 20 to 28 in long. The 26-in. size is most popular.

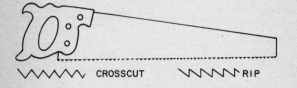

CROSSCUT   RIP

The *rip saw* is used for cutting lumber with the grain. It has five, five-and-a-half or six large teeth per inch. These have a ripping, or chisel-like, action and do almost all cutting on the forward stroke. The 26-in. blade length is standard.

Backsaws are cross-cut saws with rectangular blades held rigid by a reinforcing piece of steel along the top edge. They are used in miter boxes and for other precise cutting. The blades have 11 to 14 teeth per inch and range in length from 12 to 28 in. For most work in the home workshop, however, the 12- or 14-in. size is adequate.

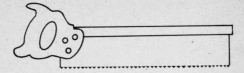

Dovetail saws resemble backsaws with straight, screwdriver-like handles. The blades are short, made of very thin steel, and have fine teeth for very careful cabinet work.

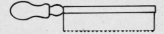

The *keyhole*, or *compass, saw* has a narrow blade that usually tapers to a small point. It is used mainly for cutting out holes and for making cuts in places where you cannot insert or manipulate a crosscut or rip saw. The blades are 10 to 14 in. long and are available with teeth of several sizes for crosscutting or ripping. Many keyhole saws are sold with interchangeable blades fitting a single handle.

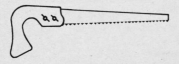

The *coping*, or *jig, saw* is designed for cutting irregular shapes in thin wood or plywood. It consists of a U-shaped steel frame with a slender, short blade inserted

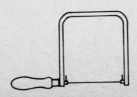

in slotted pawls. Most blades are flat strips, no more than 1/8 in. wide and with 10 to 20 teeth per inch. These can be turned in the frame so you can saw in any direction. Spiral blades also saw in any direction but do not need to be turned.

The *hacksaw* is a metalworker's tool occasionally used by a woodworker to shorten bolts, cut off heads of bolts, etc. It is an elongated, U-shaped frame in which is clamped a straight, fine-toothed blade 1/2 in. wide.

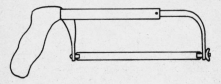

The *inside-start saw* is a Swedish tool with a very thin, flexible, rectangular blade with the front edge bowed backward. The front edge has teeth so you can turn the saw upside down and cut through the center of a board or plywood. The straight bottom edge is also toothed. The blade is 14-1/2 in. long with 14 points per inch.

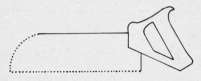

SAWHORSE. A trestle on which lumber is placed during sawing. In actual fact, however, a sawhorse is a small, portable workbench which carpenters use in many ways. It consists of a horizontal timber supported on four well braced legs.

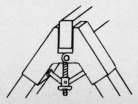

Construction of a sawhorse can be simplified by using a pair of hinged, pincer-like, steel sawhorse brackets. Two 2 x 4s are nailed into each bracket for legs. When the sawhorse is assembled, a 2 x 4 is set into the jaws of the brackets to serve as the top rail. When not in use, the sawhorse can be taken apart and the legs folded up.

SAW, PORTABLE POWER. Used primarily by carpenters outside the shop, although just as useful to the woodworker who has not installed units designed specifically for shop use.

Circular saws have revolving blades of 6-to 10-in. diameter (the most popular models use 6-, 7- or 7-1/2-in. blades). They are used for ripping or crosscutting at any angle from 90° down to 45°. The depth of the cut can be adjusted from 0 to 2-3/16 in. on a 7-in. model. Thus you can use the saw for grooving and dadoing as well as for sawing timbers.

Although circular saws are fairly heavy, they are easily operated with one hand. Blades can be quickly changed from rip to crosscut; but many carpenters use a combination blade for all wood and plywood cutting.

A *saber saw* is in effect a jig saw driven by an electric motor. It is fitted with straight, narrow blades which extend several inches below the base of the saw and move up and down in short strokes. On the best models the speed can be varied from 0 to more than 3000 strokes per minute.

The main use for saber saws, which are sometimes called bayonet saws, is in cutting circles and other irregular shapes and for making inside cuts. The blades are made with teeth of several sizes. Special round and flat files can be used in place of the saw blades to smooth and shape wood.

A reciprocating saw cuts with the same reciprocating action of a saber saw. The blade, however, projects in front of the saw and is considerably longer and wider; consequently, the tool is used for heavier work. It is particularly useful for remodeling and repairing buildings, because you can cut right through walls and floors without boring starting holes.

So-called *drill saws* and *hole saws* are actually saw blades which are used in electric drills. The former resembles a twist drill but is designed to cut a line across a board. The latter is a ring with teeth for cutting out disks rather then boring holes. It comes in 1/2- to 2-1/2-in. sizes.

SAW SET. A tool for bending saw teeth to left or right so the saw will not bind in the kerf. The same saw set is used for all hand saws and fine-toothed circular saws.

SAW, SHOP. Waist-high, stationary saw designed for precision-cutting of wood and not-too-large panels of plywood. Like other electrically driven shop tools, they are the mainstays of furniture and cabinet makers.

Bench saws, also called table saws and sometimes variety saws, are circular saws with the motor mounted beneath the work table and the blade projecting up through a slot in the table. The work is fed into the saw, which cuts on the downstroke. Blades used are 8, 9, 10 or 12 in. in diameter and are available for ripping, crosscutting or combination service. The blade tilts if you want to bevel a board.

Bench saws can also be used for dadoing and making moldings by substituting a dado head or a molding head for the saw blade.

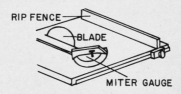

In *radial-arm saws* the motor and circular saw blade are suspended from an arm that swings out over the work table at any angle and can be adjusted up and down. In operation, the saw, which cuts on the upstroke, is pushed across the stationary work. Because the saw blade swivels from side to side and also tilts from vertical to horizontal, the machine offers great flexibility, and it can also be used with special attachments for sanding, jointing, drilling, etc. The blades range from 8- to 20-in. diameter.

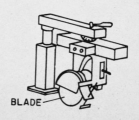

Bandsaws have narrow (1/4 to 5/8 in.) blades which form continuous loops with a length of 11 ft. The blade runs at high speed down through the work table, around through an enclosed cabinet and back to the work table again. At the cutting point, the blade is vertical; but because the table tilts, angle cuts can be made.

Bandsaws are used mainly for cutting out round and irregular shapes. But they are also used to make straight cuts in wood which is too thick for circular or radial arm saws to handle. One model, in fact, can go through wood up to 1 ft. thick.

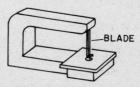

Jig, or *scroll, saws* are reciprocating saws with tiny blades used to make intricate cuts. They can cut through wood up to 4 in. thick. The table tips for beveling and mitering operations.

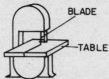

SAW VISE. A device for holding a saw blade while it is being sharpened. The vise is clamped to the workbench top and has wide jaws to hold the saw blade rigid for the better part of its length.

SCAB. In some construction, joists butted to the sides of a girder project above the top of the girder. A scab is a

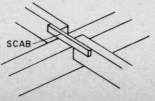

short board used to fasten opposite joists together to give a continuous flat surface across the girder.

SCAFFOLDING NAIL. See *nail*.

SCANTLING. A short timber. The studs under and over windows are scantlings.

SCARF. To form the end of a timber so it can be spliced to another timber. As a noun, scarf means the formed end of a timber. See *splice*.

SCORE. To scratch a surface with a sharp instrument or very coarse sandpaper to improve the adhesion of glue, plaster, etc.

SCORING TOOL. A sharp, knife-like tool, goosenecked at the tip, which is used for marking and lightly cutting plastic laminates and other hard composition materials.

SCRAPER. Tool with a thin, strong, straight edge used for scraping off paint, varnish and other finishes, and for smoothing wood.

The *hand scraper* is nothing more than a rectangular steel blade 5 or 6 in. long and 2-1/2 or 3 in. wide.

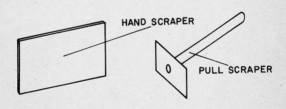

In a wood-handled *pull scraper*, a small strip of steel is clamped at right angles to the handle. The tool is used primarily when there is need for taking off a lot of wood or a thick finish, because you can exert more pressure on it than on other scrapers.

The *cabinet scraper* looks like a small spokeshave and is used in much the same way to remove small amounts of wood.

BLADE

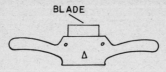

Shavehooks are small scrapers with blades of several designs for shaping wood. The blade is perpendicular to the screwdriver—like shank and handle.

SCREEN MOLDING. See *molding.*

SCREW. Although it takes more time and effort to drive a screw than to drive a nail, screws have two advantages over nails: they hold more securely and they can be removed more easily without injury to the wood.

Wood screws are usually made of steel or brass, but are also made of bronze and aluminum. The threads extend approximately two-thirds of the length of the shank. The upper third of the shank is smooth and is called the body. The head is flat, round or oval and usually has a single, straight slot. (In actuality, the so-called flat-head screw is flat on top but wedge-shaped underneath so it can be countersunk. The round-head screw is round on top but has a flat bottom, and is not countersunk. The oval-head screw is oval on top and slightly wedge-shaped beneath so it can be partially countersunk.)

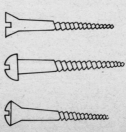

Wood screws are classified by length and diameter (gauge). Lengths range from 3/16 to 5-1/2 in. Gauge numbers start at 0, the smallest diameter, and run to 24 (approximately 3/8-in. diameter). Generally the gauge increases with the length; but screws of certain lengths are often made in several gauges. For example, 1-1/2-in., flat-head, bright-steel screws are available in ten gauges. On the other hand, no one type of screw comes in all lengths and all gauges. For example, flat-head brass screws are available in fewer sizes than blued-steel round-head screws.

In addition to screws with straight-slotted heads, there are other kinds which may be used in carpentry and woodworking. The following are the more common:

Phillips-head screws, with crossed slots, are made in many of the same sizes and types as slotted screws. But *clutchhead* and *Posidrive screws*, with slots of unusual design, come in limited sizes and types. (Screws with unusual slots in the head are more securely held in the tip of a screwdriver than those with straight slots, and can be driven down tight with less effort. They also thwart tampering better than standard screws.)

Fillister-head screws have flat or oval heads with straight sides to permit easy countersinking in an ordinary drill hole. They have straight slots.

Bung-head screws, also designed for easy countersinking, have heads which are just slightly wider than the bodies. The slots are straight.

Lag screws have large, square heads which are turned with a wrench. They are used in heavy construction.

SCREWDRIVER. Screwdrivers are made in a great many sizes; with several different tips; with wood, plastic or rubber handles; and in a few specialized designs.

The standard tool has a flat tip for driving single-slotted screws. The blades range in length from 1 in. on stubby screwdrivers to 12 in., and are normally flared to the sides just above the tip. On screwdrivers with cabinet tips, however, the blade is straight from end to end and unusually slender so that you can use it in tight places.

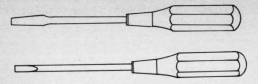

Tip widths range from 1/16 to 7/16 in. In some cases, the tip is magnetized to hold steel screws or has a spring grip for holding screws made of any metal.

Screwdrivers are also made with tips for driving screws with unusual heads. The most familiar of these is the Phillips screwdriver with a star-shaped tip ranging from 1/8 to 3/8-in. diameter. Other screwdrivers have tips for driving clutchhead and Posidrive screws.

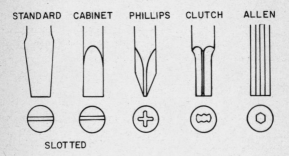

STANDARD   CABINET   PHILLIPS   CLUTCH   ALLEN

SLOTTED

Offset screwdrivers are steel rods shaped something like seahorses. They are used for driving slotted or Phillips-head screws which cannot be reached with a straight-bladed driver. An *offset ratchet screwdriver* is used for the same purpose.

Spiral ratchet screwdrivers—usually known simply as ratchet screwdrivers—are designed to speed work and make it easier. They drive or withdraw screws as you pump the handle up and down. Blades of several sizes can be used.

Another labor-saving device is a *screwdriver bit* which fits into a bit brace. It is designed for driving large slotted or Phillips-head screws. Screwdriver bits which fit variable-speed electric drills are also available.

SCREW EYE. A screw with an enclosed loop at the end opposite the point. It comes in assorted sizes up to 3-3/8 in. long. It is used primarily in a hook-and-eye combination to hold doors and windows shut.

SCREW NAIL. See *nail.*

SCRIBE. To mark and then fit a board or cabinet to an irregular surface or one that is not plumb. The marking is done with dividers or a compass. One leg is placed on the irregular surface; the other, on the board to be fitted. The tool is then run across the irregular surface from end to end in order to mark a parallel line on the board.

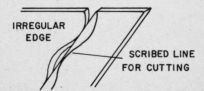

IRREGULAR
EDGE

SCRIBED LINE
FOR CUTTING

SCROLL. An ornamental carving resembling a roll of paper unrolling.

SCROLL SAW. See *saw, shop.*

SECTION DRAWING. In the working drawings for a building, the section drawing gives a cutaway view of part of the house in order to clarify its construction. For instance, a section drawing of an exterior wall depicts the inside of the wall and whatever trim, moldings, etc. are attached to the front and back.

Section drawings are labeled Section A-A, Section B-B, etc. On a floor plan or elevation, a straight line with two identical letters at the ends indicates that section drawings are included in the working drawings.

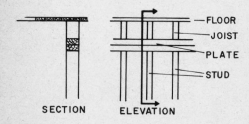

SECTION   ELEVATION

SELF-CENTERING SCREWHOLE PUNCH. See *punch.*

SHAKE. A lengthwise split between growth rings. Unlike a check, which crosses the growth rings, a shake is parallel to them. Shakes caused by high winds racking a tree are called wind shakes.

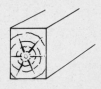

SHAKE. A thick, handsplit shingle with a very rough texture. Usually made from red cedar, shakes are produced in random widths from 4 to 14 in. and in uniform lengths of 18 and 24 in. Usually sold in bundles covering 20 sq. ft., they are graded No. 1 Handsplit-and-Resawn (with split faces and sawn backs); No. 1 Tapersplit (tapered shingles split on both sides); and No. 1 Straight-Split (split on both sides but of the same thickness from end to end).

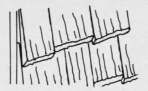

SHAPER. An electrically driven shop tool with an inter-changeable cutting head mounted on a spindle which protrudes above the center of the work table. It is used for making moldings and paneling, grooving, pattern-shaping and fluting.

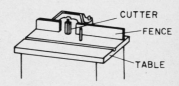

SHARPENING STONE. A small stone made of various abrasives molded and baked in an oven. It is used for the complete sharpening of some tools and the final honing of others which are rough-sharpened on a grinder.

Sharpening stones used by woodworkers have flat sides. Some stones fit easily in a pocket, but for most work, a 2 by 6-in. size is preferred. Such a stone normally has a coarse grit on one side; a finer grit on the reverse side. Although it is not essential, the stone is usually treated with oil so that it will not become clogged with bits of metal.

SHAVEHOOK. See *scraper.*

SHEATHING. The material nailed to the outside of studs and rafters which serves as the base for the finish wall material and roofing. Plywood is most often used today; but rough boards and rigid composition boards are also used. In quality construction, building paper is sandwiched between the sheathing and finish wall or roof to help further to keep out air and moisture.

SHELLAC STICK. A pencil-size stick of dried shellac used to fill holes in wood and other materials which are to be given a clear finish. The sticks come in assorted colors. When heated with a small steel spatula, the shellac melts and is dripped into the holes.

SHIM. A small strip of wood, metal, cardboard, stone— whatever is appropriate—inserted between two surfaces. The most common purpose of shims in building is to hold something in a desired position. For example, in order to level a row of base cabinets in a kitchen, it is almost always necessary to shim up some of them. Similarly, shims may be inserted under the hinge leaves in door jambs to make doors close or hang better.

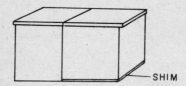

SHIM

SHINGLE. The wood shingle is a type of bevel siding much thicker at the bottom than the top. Shingles are made in random widths up to a maximum of 14 in. and are sold in bundles in uniform lengths of 16, 18 or 24 in. Each bundle covers 25 sq. ft.

Almost all shingles sold today are made of red cedar but a few are cut from eastern white cedar and redwood. Five red cedar grades are available: No. 1 Blue Label; No. 2 Red Label; No. 3 Black Label; No. 1 or No. 2 Rebutted-Rejointed; and No. 4 Undercoursing.

Red cedar shingles which are produced with deep grain-like grooves are called sidewall shakes, but they are not handsplit like true shakes.

Shingles are also made of asphalt, asbestos-cement, slate and tile.

SHINGLE NAIL. See *nail*.

SHIPLAP. A board with rabbets cut in the long edges. One rabbet faces the front side of the board; the other, the back. When the board is applied horizontally to an exterior wall, the rabbet in the upper edge faces forward. In the board next above, the bottom rabbet faces backward. Thus the two lock together to keep water from leaking in.

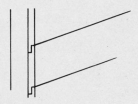

SHOE MOLDING. See *molding*.

SHOP LUMBER. See *lumber*.

SHOPSMITH. Trade name for an exceptionally versatile, large, bench-height shop tool which is used as a bench saw, vertical and horizontal drill press, lathe and disk sander. With accessories, the tool also serves several additional purposes. Power is supplied by a built-in motor and variable-speed drive.

SHORTLEAF PINE. See *pine, southern yellow*.

SHOULDER BOX. The carpenter's portable toolbox. It is open at the top and has a long, straight carrying handle. Dimensions are variable, but are roughly 32 in. long and 9 in. wide. The sides are 6 in. high. The best boxes are fitted with racks and slots to protect tools from damage.

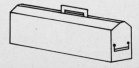

SIDING. Any material used to cover the exterior walls of a building. Lumber sidings include bevel siding, ship-lap, board and batten, vertical boards, etc. There is also a variety of plywood and hardboard sidings.

SILICONE-CARBIDE PAPER. See *sandpaper.*

SILL. The timber course on which the first-floor joists of a building rest. The timbers are bolted to the top of the foundation wall at 4-ft. intervals and extend all the way around the building. They are made of 2 x 4s, 2 x 6s or 2 x 8s placed face down. Sills are sometimes called sill plates.

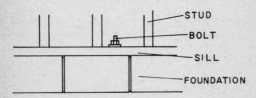

STUD
BOLT
SILL
FOUNDATION

SINGLE-ROLLER SPRING CATCH. See *catch.*

SKOTCH FASTENER. A patented metal fastener hammered across the face of a joint to reinforce it. It consists of a long, flat strap with two sharp prongs at either end.

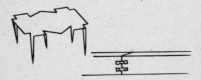

SLASH-CUT. See *grain.*

SLASH PINE. See *pine, southern yellow.*

SLEEPER. One of a series of small timbers (usually 2 x 2s) laid on a concrete subfloor to serve as the base for a wood floor.

SLICK. See *chisel, wood.*

SLIP-JOINT PLIERS. See *pliers.*

SLIPSTONE. See *oilstone.*

SMOOTH PLANE. See *plane.*

SOFFIT. The underside of a cornice, arch, beam or stairway. The vertical board or panel closing the space between kitchen wall cabinets and the ceiling is also a soffit.

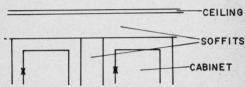

SOFT AND HARDBOARD PLANE. See *plane.*

SOFT-FACE HAMMER. See *hammer.*

SOFTWOOD. A softwood is a tree with needle-like leaves. It is also the lumber cut from such a tree. Pine and spruce are softwoods. By contrast, oak and hickory are hardwoods. Generally, as the words imply, softwoods are softer than hardwoods; but in several cases they are not. Southern yellow pine, for instance, is much harder than basswood, although the latter is called a hardwood.

SOLE. A horizontal timber (usually a 2 x 4), at the base of a wall, to which the studs are nailed. Commonly called a sole plate or wall plate.

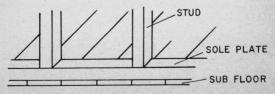

SPACKLE. Also called spackling compound, this is a plaster-like material used to fill holes in painted wood and also in plaster and gypsum board. One type of spackle is a dry powder which is mixed with water. The other type, made with vinyl, comes in a can ready to use.

Until recently, spackle could be used only inside a building. New mixtures are now available for exterior and interior work.

SPADE. See *gouge*.

SPAN. The distance between the supports under joists, beams, girders and trusses. The allowable span for such timbers is limited by the material of which they are made, their size, how many of them are used, and the load upon them.

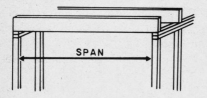

SPECIFICATIONS. Typewritten or sometimes printed information specifying the materials, etc., that are to be used in constructing a building, bookcase, piece of furniture, etc.

SPIKE. Large common nail used for fastening timbers. Spikes range from 6 to 12 in. long. Most have flat heads but a few have oval heads.

SPINDLE SANDER. See *sanding machine*.

SPIRAL RATCHET SCREWDRIVER. See *screwdriver*.

SPLICE. When two timbers are joined together end to end to form, in effect, a single long timber, they are said to be spliced.

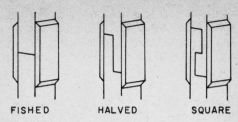

FISHED   HALVED   SQUARE

The simplest splice to make when the spliced timber will be subject to compression (pressure from the two ends) is called the *fished splice*. In this, the ends of the short timbers are squared and butted together, and then secured by boards called fishplates nailed, screwed or bolted to the sides.

A better splice for compression is called the *halved splice*. This is made by notching the ends of both timbers as for a half lap (see *joint*), then attaching fishplates to the sides.

For a timber that will be under tension (pulling apart) a *square splice* is the simplest joint. This is similar to a halved splice except that both timbers have slightly L-shaped notches so that they lock together and cannot be pulled apart.

Various other ways of scarfing (forming) the ends of timbers for tension splices are used, but most involve more complicated cutting and fitting than the square splice.

SPLICEPLATE. See *fishplate*.

SPLINE. A small strip of wood used as a fastener. A spline is sometimes used to strengthen a miter joint. See *joint*. Very long splines are often used to hold the edges of window-screen mesh in grooves in the frame.

SPLIT. A lengthwise crack in lumber caused by the tearing apart of the wood cells. As opposed to checks, which are caused by the natural shrinkage of wood as it is seasoned, splits are usually man-made. However, there is no difference in the appearance of a split and a check.

SPOKESHAVE. A plane-like tool with a short bottom to permit planing of the edges of cut-out pieces of wood and also used to dress rounded pieces. It has two handles on either side of the cutting blade. The bottom is either flat for use on cut-out pieces with long sweeping curves or convex for use on pieces with short sweeping curves.

A spokeshave is usually pushed away from you but can be pulled toward you.

SPRINGWOOD. The woody growth made by trees during the early part of the growing season. See *summerwood*.

SPRING CLAMP. See *clamp*.

SPRUCE. A softwood with a close, straight grain which is quite easy to work. Eastern spruce wood is pink to reddish in color; Englemann spruce is off-white. All spruce lumber has unusual strength in relation to its light weight. It is used primarily in construction. Eastern spruce also goes into musical instruments.

SQUARE. One hundred square feet. Roofing materials are figured in squares.

SQUARE. L-shaped device used mainly for checking the squareness of lumber and for measuring and marking right angles, but not limited to these operations.

The *try and miter square* is the smallest square. It has a steel blade 6 or 8 in. long and a thick handle 4 or 5-1/2 in. long. One edge of the handle has a corner beveled to 45° for use in mitering.

The *try square* is similar but lacks the bevel in the handle. The handle is about two-thirds as long as the blade, which ranges from 6 to 12 in. Together with the try and miter square, this is the basic instrument for testing wood for squareness and smoothness, and for indicating 90° saw cuts on boards.

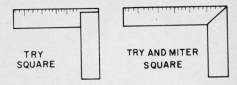

TRY
SQUARE

TRY AND MITER
SQUARE

Combination squares have a steel handle which slides along the blade and is useful not only for marking right angles but also for making longitudinal lines on boards and for finding the depth of holes. In addition, the handle is shaped for marking 45° angles, and contains one or two spirit levels for leveling and plumbing surfaces. Some squares even incorporate a tiny scratch awl.

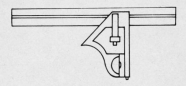

Another even more versatile square is called an *All-N-One measuring tool*. It is used as a square, marking gauge, level, plumb, protractor, depth gauge, beam compass, stud marker, screw gauge, dowel gauge and nail gauge.

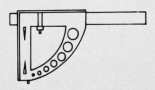

Flat squares are simpler devices intermediate between try squares and framing squares. They are made of one piece of flat steel cut in an L.

Of all the squares, the *framing*, or *carpenter's, square* is the most important and useful, although it, too, is simply a big, flat, L-shaped piece of steel. The long blade, called the body, measures 24 by 2 in. The short blade, called the tongue, is 16 by 1-1/2 in. Both the body and tongue are marked with graduations for making measurements and with special tables.

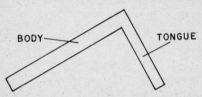

BODY — TONGUE

Carpenters use framing squares for such specialized tasks as measuring and cutting rafters and braces, figuring board measure, converting timbers from squares to octagons, calculating proportions, finding the circumference and center of a circle, and laying out ellipses, miters and hopper joints.

Also see *center square*.

SQUARE FOOT. The standard unit of measure for lumber material 1/2 in. thick or less, such as siding and plywood. A square foot is 12 in. wide by 1 ft. long. The term surface foot is sometimes used instead of square foot.

SQUARE SPLICE. See *splice*.

STANBRITE. A polishing belt for use in belt sanders. It is made of nylon mesh impregnated with a very fine abrasive which produces an ultra-smooth finish on wood, plywood and other materials. Because the mesh has large openings, sawdust falls through and does not clog the belt.

STAPLER. A staple-driving tool used to fasten thin, soft materials such as asphalt roofing, building paper and upholstery to wood. To use it, you simply hold it flat against the material to be tacked down and squeeze the handle. Some staplers can drive staples ranging from 1/4 to 9/16 in. long.

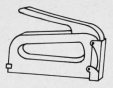

STAR DRILL. A long, straight tool of hardened steel with a star-shaped point. It is used to drill holes by hand in concrete, brick and other masonry. You hold the drill loosely in your hand against the masonry and strike the back end with a hammer. The drill must be turned constantly to make a round hole. Different sizes are available.

This tool has been obsoleted to some extent by carbide-tipped bits made for electric drills, but it is still more efficient than the latter when you are drilling stone and concrete made with very coarse aggregate.

STATIC LOAD. See *load.*

STEEL WOOL. Pads of fine, tough steel threads used for smoothing wood, plywood and metal and for rubbing down varnish and other clear finishes. They come in seven grades ranging from No. 0000, the finest, to No. 3, the coarsest.

Bronze wool is substituted for steel wool if the wood is to be exposed to water.

STILE. The vertical, top-to-bottom side pieces of a door. Also the two side members of a window sash.

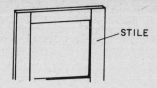

STIRRUP. A metal support for a beam or joist. See *hanger*.

STOCK. Standard; carried in stock. Almost all lumber materials are produced and sold in stock sizes, such as 2- by 4-in. timbers and 4- by 8-ft. panels of plywood. The word is also applied to such things as kitchen cabinets, millwork, windows, doors, moldings, etc.

STOP. Any device which restricts the motion of some moving part of a structure. For example, the narrow strips of wood on the jambs in a doorway are stops. Similarly, the strips that keep double-hung windows from falling out of their frames are stops.

Other stops are rubber-tipped metal bumpers used to keep doors from banging against walls.

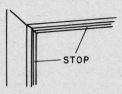

STOVE BOLT. See *bolt*.

STRAIGHT-EDGE. Any long, absolutely straight strip of wood or metal used for marking straight lines and checking lumber, surfaces, etc.

STRAP HINGE. See *hinge*.

STRINGER. A large, horizontal timber connecting up-right posts in a building and supporting a floor. Stringers of this type are at least 5 in. thick. Their width is at least 2 in. greater than their thickness.

A stringer is also the slanting timber that supports a stair. This kind of stringer is normally made out of lumber 2 in. thick. See *housed stringer*.

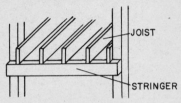

STRIP FLOORING. See *flooring*.

STRUCTURAL LUMBER. See *lumber*.

STRUT. A structural piece designed to keep two other pieces separated. A strut, in other words, is a load- or pressure-resisting device. In a truss, for example, struts nailed between the top and bottom chords are designed to resist the load on the rafters. Illustrated at *truss*.

STUD. One of the upright timbers in a framed wall to which sheathing, gypsum board, plaster lath, etc. is nailed. Studs are usually cut from 2 x 4s but in certain situations may be made of 2 x 3s or 2 x 6s. They are normally spaced 16 in. on centers but are often spaced 12 or 24 in. on centers.

A short stud installed under or over a window is called a cripple stud.

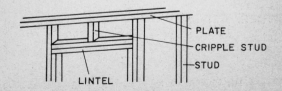

STUD DRIVER. A tool for driving a special type of hardened steel nail, called a stud, into a masonry wall. It is used for fastening furring strips, shelf brackets, etc. to such walls. The stud is placed in the nose of the driver. You then hold the driver against the wall and strike a trigger in the back with a hammer. A piston inside the tool concentrates the force of the blow and drives the stud easily into even a poured concrete wall.

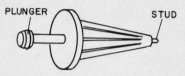

PLUNGER   STUD

STUD FINDER. A small magnetic gadget which is held against a wall to indicate the location of nails holding the studs.

SUBFLOORING. The material nailed to floor joists which serves as the base for the finish flooring. Subflooring is almost always made of plywood, but rough boards can be used.

SUGAR PINE. See *pine, white.*

SUMMERWOOD. Trees grow by forming annual rings of wood just under the bark. If you examine these carefully, you may see that each ring has two parts—a light-colored inner part and a darker-colored outer part. The inner part is known as the springwood because it was formed early in the growing season. The outer part, called the summerwood or sometimes the autumnwood, was formed later in the growing season.

Summerwood is stronger than springwood because it is composed of smaller cells with thicker walls; consequently, when selecting a softwood such as Douglas fir for critical structural purposes, it is advisable to pick out timbers with a high proportion of summerwood. Such a wood is called a dense wood.

SURFACE FOOT. Alternate term for square foot.

SURFACE LATCH. See *latch*.

SURFORM TOOL. Tool for rapidly shaping and removing wood, as well as plastics and soft metals. The cutting edge, which has a general resemblance to the coarser sides of a kitchen grater, is made up of hundreds of tiny, sharp blades which take off wood like a plane and pass the chips back up through holes to the top of the tool. The holes also permit you to see the exact area you are cutting.

One Surform tool is shaped like a large, flat file. A ribbed section on the front of the body permits two-hand use. A round file 5/8 in. in diameter is also available. Both tools are used in place of a rasp for shaping operations.

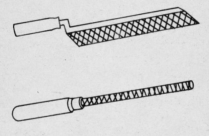

Two tools shaped like planes—one of pocket-size—are made for working on larger surfaces. There are also two-way tools with a rear handle which adjusts so you can use them either as files or as planes.

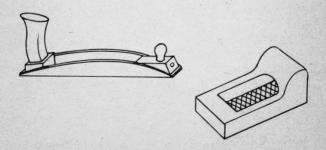

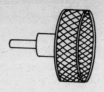

A drum-shaped Surform tool for use in electric drills or drill presses is designed for heavy-duty shaping.

All the tools have replaceable blades.

SWEDISH PUTTY. An obsolete wood filler made with dry spackle powder, water and varnish. It is waterproof.

SYCAMORE. A hard, heavy, reddish-brown hardwood used in furniture parts.

T

TACK. Very sharp, short, tapering fastening device with large flat head. Because tacks are easy to pull, they are used for fastening down flexible materials which require fairly frequent replacement. Made of steel, copper or aluminum, they have a maximum length of a little less than 1 in.

TACK PULLER. A screwdriver-shaped tool with a slot in the tip for pulling tacks.

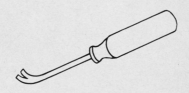

TAIL. Adjective applied to a relatively short joist or beam which butts against a header.

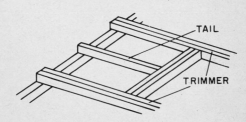

TAKE DOWN. To reduce the thickness or width of a piece of wood with a cutting tool such as a plane or drawknife.

TAKE OFF. To copy down measurements on a plan.

TAKE UP. To shorten or take the slack out of something.

TANG. The slender projecting part of a tool which is inserted in a handle and holds the two pieces together.

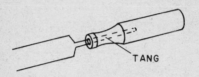

TANGUILE. One of several hardwoods sold as Philippine mahogany.

TAPE. The retractable steel measuring tape that has replaced the folding wood rule in a number of toolboxes. These tapes are made in 6-, 8-, 10-, 12-, 16-, 20- and 25-ft. lengths. See *rule*.

Steel tapes for measuring large spaces during construction of buildings come in 25-, 50-, 75- and 100-ft. lengths. They are closed with a small handcrank.

TASMANIAN OAK. See *eucalyptus*.

TEAK. A heavy, strong, medium hard wood which turns from golden yellow when cut to a handsome brown with dark stripes. It is fragrant, has excellent dimensional stability and is one of the most durable woods. It is used in fine furniture, paneling, flooring and shipbuilding.

TEMPLATE. See *templet.*

TEMPLET. A pattern made of thin wood or metal which is used as a guide in forming work.

TENON. A projection formed on the end of a piece of wood which is then inserted in a mortise of the same size. See *joint.*

TEXTURE. As applied to wood, "texture" can be used interchangeably with "grain". A fine-textured wood is one with a fine grain. A coarse-textured wood is one with a coarse or open grain.

T HINGE. See *hinge.*

THRESHOLD. The strip of wood or metal under a door.

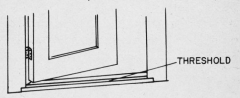

THRESHOLD

THUMB LATCH. See *latch.*

THUYA. Very fragrant wood from an Asian relative of the arborvitae. The burl is used in inlay work and for making art objects. It is heavy and brittle; varies from almost black to light brown. The finest burl resembles a peacock feather.

TIE BEAM. A timber that ties together parts of a building. For example, the collar beams which link rafters in the roof are tie beams.

TIGERWOOD. Also called African walnut. An easily worked furniture and paneling wood with a gold to gray-brown background and black ribbon stripes.

TOENAIL. To drive a nail on a slant through the end or edge of one piece of lumber into another. Studs are toenailed at the ends to soles and plates because it is the simplest and usually the only way to fasten them. Similarly, strip flooring is toenailed through the tongue edge to the subfloor in order to conceal the nailheads. Illustrated at *joint*.

TOGGLE BOLT. A device for attaching things to hollow walls which will not hold nails or screws. In the most common type, the nut on the bolt has two wings which are actuated by a tiny spring. To use the fastener, a hole big enough to receive the nut with the wings folded is drilled through the wall. The bolt is then slipped through the object to be hung; the nut is attached to it and is pushed through the wall. As the bolt is tightened, it draws the nut, with wings now open, up tight against the inside surface of the wall. Toggle bolts range from 2 to 6 in. long.

TONGUE AND GROOVE. Often abbreviated T & G. A board with a projecting rib, or tongue, along one of the long edges and a channel, or groove, along the opposite edge in a corresponding position. The tongue of one board is designed to slip into the groove of an adjoining board, thus making for a more rigid, moisture-resistant surface. Illustrated at *joint*.

TOOLBOX. A box in which tools are kept. The design is pretty much a personal matter dictated by what tools you own, how much space you have for the box, etc. But the one point the careful craftsman never forgets is that the box must be designed and fitted so that the tools will not bang against and damage one another.

When out on the job, carpenters keep their tools in shoulder boxes. See *shoulder box*.

TOUCH CATCH. See *catch*.

TOURNIQUET. A homemade device to pull together parts of a structure—most commonly a piece of furniture—when they are being glued. It consists of a stout cord or rope tied around the parts (which should be padded to keep the cord from cutting into them). A stick of wood or screwdriver blade is then inserted between the parallel lines and twisted round and round in windlass fashion until the joints are tight.

T PLATE. A flat, T-shaped steel mending plate for strengthening joints. It is available in sizes from 3 by 3 in. to 6 by 6 in. It is sometimes called a T iron.

TRAMMEL POINTS. Sharp steel pins that are attached to a straight piece of wood and used to draw large circles and curves. Compare *radial bar*.

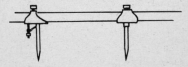

TRANSOM CATCH. See *catch*.

TREAD. The surface stepped on when climbing stairs.

TRIM. The exposed wood and sometimes metal pieces inside and outside a building which are used to cover joints or add decoration. They include the frames around doors and windows, baseboards, moldings, soffits, etc.

TRIMMER. The floor joist or beam to which a header is attached. Illustrated at *tail.*

TRIMMING PLANE. See *plane.*

TRUSS. A large roof-framing member composed of several timbers, which is assembled on the ground or in a shop and then set into place. Truss design depends on the design of the roof and the space the truss will span. For example, a truss for a gable roof is a large triangle made up of two fairly short pieces that serve as the rafters and a long piece that is the ceiling joist. The large timbers, called chords, are usually held together and braced with struts, gussets and fishplates.

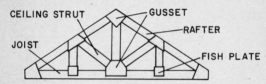

Because trusses are put together on the ground, they simplify and usually reduce the cost of roof framing. They can be used in much wider spans than conventional roof framing; thus they often eliminate the need for bearing walls in the center of a house.

TRY AND MITER SQUARE. See *square.*

TRY SQUARE. See *square.*

TULIPWOOD. A Brazilian inlay wood which, in its best form, is both rosy-red and creamy-colored. It is extremely hard and difficult to work, but when finished has a beautiful glassy texture.

TUPELO. Sometimes known as tupelo gum or sap gum, tupelo is a medium-weight hardwood. Brownish-gray in color and of moderate strength, it is used in furniture parts.

TURNBUCKLE. A device that is inserted between the ends of two metal rods or wires to pull them together and thus to put tension on the parts to which they are connected. A door brace used to straighten sagging screen doors has a turnbuckle. The brace is attached to diagonally opposite corners of a door. When the turn-buckle at the middle is screwed tight, the sagging corner of the door is raised.

TURNBUTTON. A simple locking device consisting of a short piece of metal or wood pivoted on a screw.

TURNING. A piece of wood that has been shaped on a lathe.

TWIST DRILL. See *bit*.

U

UPRIGHT. Any vertical timber in a structure.

UTILITY KNIFE. A knife with a slot cut in one end of a rounded handle for a razor-like blade which, in some models, retracts. As it protrudes from the handle, the blade is triangular in shape and provides about 1 in. of cutting edge. For this reason, the knife cannot be used for whittling but is excellent for marking (it is also called a marking knife) and slicing through veneers, building paper, resilient flooring, etc.

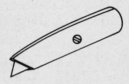

UTILITY VISE. See *vise*.

V

VALLEY RAFTER. See *rafter*.

VEINER. See *gouge*.

VENEER. A very thin sheet of beautiful wood glued to a base of inferior wood. The composite material thus created is often loosely referred to as a wood veneer.

Since a wood veneer of, say, mahogany costs less than a solid piece of mahogany of the same thickness, wood veneers are used extensively in furniture and cabinet work to reduce the cost of the finished pieces. Another purpose of veneering is to stretch the supply of rare woods.

VISE. Device for holding wood stationary while you work on it at the workbench. Small clamp-on and vacuum-base vises are available; but for anyone who considers himself a woodworker, a large, permanently mounted vise is essential.

The most popular type, called a *woodworker's vise*, is installed under the front edge of a workbench at one end. The jaws are flush with the bench. In the largest model, they are 4 in. high, 10 in. wide and have a maximum opening of 12 in. You can slide the movable jaw in and out by hand; to tighten or loosen it, you turn the handle controlling a long screw.

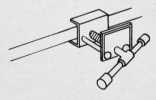

Bench vises are more suitable for the metalworker than the woodworker, but can be used by the latter if the jaws are padded. The vises are bolted to the top of the workbench. The jaws on the largest models have a maximum opening of 6 in. Some models can be swiveled from side to side and locked in place.

A completely different device is a *utility vise* which is used to hold work at drill presses, grinders, etc. It is a portable unit with a flat base which, in some cases, has a tilting or swiveling feature to permit you to position work as necessary without fear of its toppling. The largest vise has jaws that open to 4 in.

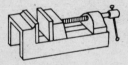

V TOOL. See *gouge*.

W

WALNUT. Cut from black walnut trees, this is the out-standing furniture and cabinet wood native to the United States. It is also used in paneling. It is heavy, hard, strong and tough. The heartwood is light to dark brown; the sapwood, very light brown. The grain is straight. The wood is relatively easy to work and takes a beautiful finish.

WANE. When a piece of lumber is missing wood along the edge or at a corner, the defect is called a wane.

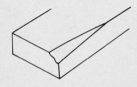

WARP. As a noun, a warp is a bend or twist in a piece of wood. As a verb, warp means to bend or twist. Warping results from the uneven shrinkage of wood cells when wood dries out. Warps are classified according to their shapes as bows, crooks, cups or twists.

WASHER. Metal washers of two types are used with nuts and bolts. The primary purpose of flat, punched-hole washers is to keep bolt heads and nuts from pulling through or marring the wood pieces which they join together. They may also be used, in effect, to shorten bolts. Sizes range from 9/16-in. outside diameter (1/4-in. inside diameter) to 5-1/2-in. outside diameter (3-1/8-in. inside diameter).

Lock washers are designed to prevent loosening of nuts bearing on a metal surface or on flat washers. The commonest type of washer is an incomplete circle of steel in which the ends lie in different planes. It comes with inside diameters up to 3/4 in. Another common lock washer is a complete, slightly saucer-shaped steel ring with a toothed edge.

WATER PUTTY. See *putty*.

WEB CLAMP. See *clamp*.

WHETSONE. See *sharpening stone*.

WHITE OAK. See *oak*.

WHITE POCKET. A small white pocket made in wood by a fungus disease. It is also called white speck. Although it mars the appearance of wood, it does not affect its utility.

WIDE-THROW HINGE. See *hinge*.

WIGGLE NAIL. See *corrugated fastener*.

WING DIVIDERS. See *dividers*.

WIRE NAIL. See *nail*.

WITH THE GRAIN. A term used when you are working lumber longitudinally—more or less parallel with the grain—rather than across it at an angle.

When using a tool such as a plane or drawknife, it is possible to work with the grain and yet against it because the grain in a piece of lumber rarely parallels the edges of the piece exactly. If the grain happens to slope upward toward your plane, you are likely to gouge or splinter the wood.

Accordingly, "working with the grain" also means moving a tool in the same direction as the grain's upward slope.

WOOD DOUGH. A wood filler made with wood fibers. It is available in assorted colors.

WOOD FILLER. See *filler.*

WOOD PRESERVATIVE. A liquid to make wood and plywood more resistant to rot and attack by termites and similar insects. By stabilizing the moisture content in wood, a preservative also increases dimensional stability and makes the wood more warp-resistant.

The most effective wood preservatives are creosote or pentachlorophenol and copper naphthanate in a heavy oil vehicle. However, these make it impossible to paint the wood. Wood to be painted must be treated with pentachlorophenol or copper naphthanate in a light oil vehicle or with a water-dissolved preservative.

For complete penetration of a preservative, wood should be pressure-treated at a mill. Application by dipping or with a brush, roller or spray gun is less effective but nevertheless helpful.

WOOD PUTTY. See *putty.*

WOOD SCREW. See *screw.*

WOODWORK. All the exposed wood inside a building except the floors, doors and window sashes.

WOODWORKER'S VISE. See *vise.*

WORKBENCH. A sturdy table serving as a multi-purpose work surface for the woodworker. The design varies with the man who builds the bench. As a very general rule, however, benches are about 32 in. high, 5 ft. long and 2 ft. wide. A woodworker's vise is installed at one end. Several holes are drilled in a line down the middle of the bench to hold a bench stop.

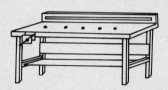

WORKING DRAWING. The completed plan from which a carpenter or craftsman works. Working drawings for houses include floor plans, elevations, special detail drawings and section drawings.

WRENCH. A tool made in numerous designs and with many purposes. But a carpenter or woodworker can get by easily with a single open-end, or angle, wrench. This has jaws adjustable to a maximum opening of 1 in.

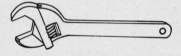

Y

YARD LUMBER. See *lumber.*

YELLOW PINE. See *pine, southern yellow.*

YELLOW POPLAR. A soft, creamy-brown hardwood cut from massive American trees known as yellow poplars, tulip poplars or tuliptrees. The wood has an indistinct grain. It is not overly strong but is easily worked. Its main use is in furniture.

YEW. A very hard, fine-grained, heavy wood with white or creamy sapwood and brown heartwood. It is used for tool handles and similar instruments as well as in cabinet work.

Z

ZEBRAWOOD. A moderately hard, West African cabinet wood with a straw-colored background and parallel brown stripes. In some wood the stripes are thin and wavy; in others, wide and very straight. The wood has a rather open grain. The pores are shiny inside.